CONTENTS UNIT 29

General Introduction   5

PART 1 TED HUGHES

1 *The Hawk in the Rain*   7

2 *Lupercal*   16

3 *Wodwo*   23

4 *Crow*   25

5 Conclusion   27

Suggestions for Further Work on Ted Hughes   28

Further Reading   29

Select Criticism and References   29

PART 2 SYLVIA PLATH

1 The Myth   31

2 'Metaphors'   33

3 *The Colossus*   38

4 *Ariel*   46

5 Conclusion   53

Suggestions for Further Work on Sylvia Plath   55

Further Reading   55

Select Criticism and References   56

THE OPEN UNIVERSITY

Arts : A Third Level Course
Twentieth Century Poetry

Unit 29

TED HUGHES
SYLVIA PLATH

Prepared by Dennis Walder for the Course Team

**University of
Hertfordshire**

Cover *Giorgio de Chirico* Disquieting Muses (*Mattioli Collection, Photo: Scala* © *1976 SPADEM Paris*). *See page 43 of the unit.*

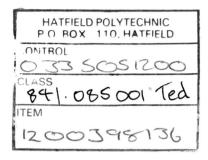
The Open University Press
Walton Hall, Milton Keynes
MK7 6AA

First published 1976. Reprinted 1977, 1979

Designed by the Media Development Group of the Open University.

Printed in Great Britain by
EYRE AND SPOTTISWOODE LIMITED
AT GROSVENOR PRESS PORTSMOUTH

ISBN 0 335 05120 0

This text forms part of an Open University course. The complete list of units in the course appears at the end of this text.

For general availability of supporting material referred to in this text, please write to Open University Educational Enterprises Limited, 12 Cofferidge Close, Stony Stratford, Milton Keynes, MK11 1BY, Great Britain.

Further information on Open University courses may be obtained from the Admissions Office, The Open University, P.O. Box 48, Walton Hall, Milton Keynes, MK7 6AB.

1.3

UNIT 29

GENERAL INTRODUCTION

One of the most important aims of this course is to sharpen and extend your reading of poetry *now*, in our present condition. As you will no doubt have already discovered, one can respond with the pleasure of immediate recognition ('Yes, this is what I feel') to the poetry of fifty or sixty years ago, to the poetry of Hardy, Yeats or Eliot, not to mention any of their predecessors, such as Hopkins or even Browning; but there is, I think, a unique potential in the poetry of our own time, of the present day, to reach us and move us – not only by exploring our everyday social and political preoccupations, although this is certainly valuable, but also by touching the deeper springs of fear and hope which lie beneath them, and which we dimly sense within ourselves as we live on into the last quarter of the twentieth century. You may recall from the discussion of F. R. Leavis in Unit 19 that it was Leavis's insistent belief that contemporary verse should be studied as the finest, most concentrated and powerful expression of current modes of feeling and experience. It was this belief which largely informed his defence of Eliot's work in *New Bearings in English Poetry*, and the same belief informs this unit. A sincere concern for poetry must include an interest in contemporary verse, in what is happening *now*.

Two poets remarkable for the fierce power and concentration with which they have tapped the unique potential of poetry of our own time, and who have been widely recognized as among the most distinguished poets of our generation writing in English to do so, are Ted Hughes and Sylvia Plath, the subjects of this unit. Hughes, a Yorkshireman born on 17 August 1930 in Mytholmroyd in the West Riding, is still very much an active poet. Even as I write this (in 1976), critics struggle over his latest sequence of poems, *Cave Birds*, which had its first public performance at the Ilkley Literature Festival on 30 May 1975, but which is not yet widely available in print. For this reason alone, one needs to be prepared to re-interpret his poetry all the time: no definitive judgements can be passed on a body of work not yet complete. In a sense, the same is true of Sylvia Plath's poetry, although she died by suicide early in 1963. For much of her greatest work has come out posthumously, and not all of it has yet appeared.[1] There is another point, one which applies to all contemporary poets: they are so close to us in time and in what they write about, that there is a special danger that we will slot them prematurely into some literary-critical category before we have really listened to what they have to say to us. While it is part of their importance and attraction that present-day poets express our current mood, this also leads to a blurring of their outlines, making them hard to define or 'place'. Judgements about such writers should therefore always be treated with more care than we are used to applying to remarks about the giants of the past. I have tried to be careful about this myself. But I hope you will remember this in reading what I have to say in the unit. Any conclusions I come to must be taken as provisional.

My aim here is fairly straightforward: to identify and introduce to you the poetry of Ted Hughes and Sylvia Plath, mainly by discussing in some detail a selection of poems (unfortunately but of necessity a small selection) from their most important collections. The books I deal with are as follows: Ted Hughes, *The Hawk in the Rain* (1957), *Lupercal* (1960) and *Wodwo* (1967), with some reference to *Crow* (1970, but

---

[1]Some previously unpublished and uncollected poems may be found in *The Art of Sylvia Plath*, ed. Newman, Appendix; a complete collected works is 'planned' (p 319).

incomplete); Sylvia Plath, *The Colossus* (1960) and *Ariel* (1965). Most of the Hughes poems I deal with or refer to may be found in his *Selected Poems 1957–1967* (1972, available in Faber paperback), although any of you interested in following up what I have to say ought to try and read the poems in the original collections, as they were written as part of a series almost from the beginning of Hughes's career. I have concentrated on poetry rather than personality, difficult though this is with writers as 'personal' as Hughes and Plath.

Basically, I look at both writers as inheritors of the 'modernist' tradition of seeking new poetic forms to do justice to a radical view of life, a view which explores the deeper levels of awareness ignored by poets more concerned with the everyday surfaces of individual or social behaviour, poets such as those embalmed in the anthology *New Lines* in 1956 for their suspicion of large gestures and strong feelings, and subsequently called the Movement (the best of these of course did not remain tied down by the limitations of this attitude, as you will have seen from Unit 28 on Philip Larkin).[2] But my overriding objective has been simply to look at what seems both characteristic and lasting in the works of Hughes and Plath, taking as my starting point in both cases a single, probably typical poem from their earlier works and trying to observe how it functions and what it is about.

Sylvia Plath is an American poet. She was born on 27 October 1932 in Boston, Massachusetts, of Austrian and German parents, and lived in America until she won a Fulbright scholarship to Cambridge in 1955, where she met Ted Hughes, whom she married in June 1956. Hughes, the son of a carpenter, went up to Cambridge in 1951 to read English, after attending Mexborough Grammar School and doing two years National Service in the RAF. He changed to Archaeology and Anthropology before graduating in 1954. Thereafter he did some schoolteaching and took various odd jobs, including working in a zoo, before meeting his wife. Sylvia Plath had had a brilliant academic career before coming to England and had already shown signs of serious mental disturbance, including one suicide attempt. But the marriage looked set to produce a remarkable creative partnership. Hughes had published little, although his wife had published poems in America as an undergraduate, yet it was soon clear how things might develop: Sylvia Plath began to submit Hughes's poems to magazines, several were published, and during 1957 Hughes made a recording of some of Yeats's poems (he knew Yeats by heart long before this) and one of his own for the BBC Third Programme; the same year Sylvia Plath had several poems accepted by *Poetry* magazine (Chicago).

From 1957 to 1959, the two lived in the United States in an intensively creative writing partnership, teaching at first, but then writing poetry full-time, before returning to England to settle. Three years later their separation was followed by Sylvia Plath's tragic death in her London flat. The couple had two children, Frieda and Nicholas. Inevitably, there is a strong temptation to link their poetry, which is in some ways closely related. But it is a relationship of contrast. As Sylvia Plath remarked of their literary life together in America: 'We do criticise each other's work, but we write poems that are as distinct and different as our fingerprints themselves must be'[3] – a characteristically precise and intimate image. So I deal with Ted Hughes and Sylvia Plath separately here, as befits their achievement.

[2]On the Movement, see Press, *A Map of Modern English Verse*, Chapter 15, especially the comments of Charles Tomlinson.

[3]'Four Young Poets', *Mademoiselle*, January 1959, p 35, quoted in Eileen Aird, *Sylvia Plath*, p 10.

PART 1   TED HUGHES

1   THE HAWK IN THE RAIN

1.1   To begin with, I'd like you to read the following poem carefully two or three times, and at least once aloud.[1] It is taken from Ted Hughes's first collection of poems, *The Hawk in the Rain* (1957). If it is familiar to you – as it may be, for Hughes is a heavily anthologized poet – try nevertheless to read it with a fresh eye and ear.

> *The Thought-Fox*
>
> I imagine this midnight moment's forest:
> Something else is alive
> Beside the clock's loneliness
> And this blank page where my fingers move.
>
> Through the window I see no star:
> Something more near
> Though deeper within darkness
> Is entering the loneliness:
>
> Cold, delicately as the dark snow,
> A fox's nose touches twig, leaf;
> Two eyes serve a movement, that now
> And again now, and now, and now
>
> Sets neat prints into the snow
> Between trees, and warily a lame
> Shadow lags by stump and in hollow
> Of a body that is bold to come
>
> Across clearings, an eye,
> A widening deepening greenness,
> Brilliantly, concentratedly,
> Coming about its own business
>
> Till, with a sudden sharp hot stink of fox
> It enters the dark hole of the head.
> The window is starless still; the clock ticks,
> The page is printed.

■   What are your immediate impressions? What does the poem seem to be about?

Discussion

1.2   My initial response to this poem was of astonishment at the sharp feeling it evokes of the physical presence of a fox, brought alive as I read it by the clear and precise details of the animal's appearance and manner, its nose 'delicately' touching 'twig, leaf', its paws setting 'neat prints into the snow', with a movement reflected in the rhythmical, hypnotic repetition of 'now/And again now, and now, and now', in the third stanza. The poem seems to be about a fox. Yet as Hughes himself pointed

---

[1]You may hear Hughes reading some poems from *Crow* (not discussed in this Unit) in Radio Programme 15. See the Broadcast Notes.

out in talking about 'the first "animal" poem I ever wrote', this is 'about a fox, obviously enough, but a fox that is both a fox and not a fox'. The title alone tells us as much, and moreover the poem begins 'I imagine', which implies a speaker, a mind which the fox can inhabit as metaphor. Perhaps most important in one's initial impression of the poem, is the dramatic double-take one experiences on arriving at the last line, when one realizes that the page is indeed printed, and lies before one's eyes. The 'neat prints' of the fox's paws have become the letters and words describing them. Thus you have been made to share the pleasurable shock of the emergence of a poem, a sharing which must be of importance to a man who visualizes himself as isolated in the dark 'loneliness' (the word is repeated twice) of midnight, awaiting inspiration.

Figure 1 Ted Hughes (Camera Press. Photo: Fay Goodwin)

Simply, then, this is a poem about the writing of a poem. A traditional subject, one might say, remembering, for example, Coleridge's 'Dejection: An Ode'; and written, as it happens, in the familiar situation of the Romantic poet, for it is the product of an inspired recall of childhood memory which came to Hughes late one night in his dreary London lodgings after a year without writing, rather as the remembered forms of youthful perception sustained Wordsworth 'in lonely rooms, and mid the din/Of towns and cities' ('Tintern Abbey', lines 26–7), bringing restorative creative impulses. Yet what about the form? It is simple (though unmistakably modern), consisting of a tight structure of four-line stanzas common to Hughes's early verse, subtly half-rhyming, and based on a four-stress line of eight or ten syllables, with the exception of the last, climactic line, which punches its dramatic point home with only two strong alliterative stresses.

But I wonder, if, in the end, the poem *is* all that simple and straightforward?

I wouldn't want to make any very large claims for it, although to catch the moment of imaginative inspiration in such a way, a way most readers should find both accurate and memorable, at least justifies Hughes's claim that 'long after I am gone, as long as a copy of the poem exists, every time anyone reads it the fox will get up somewhere out in the darkness and come walking towards them' – a claim made in his brilliant and revealing little anthology of poems and talks, *Poetry in the Making* (pp 19–20), based on a radio series about the reading and writing of poetry for schools, and the source also of his remarks above on 'The Thought-Fox'. It is, I think, significant that Hughes chose 'The Thought-Fox' as the first of his works to discuss in *Poetry in the Making*: it may have been because of its simple accessibility, its immediacy and vividness of surface, although this is typical of his early verse (before *Wodwo* and *Crow*); it may also have been because it was, as he says, his first 'animal' poem, although, obviously, not his first poem; but my feeling is that with 'The Thought-Fox' Hughes discovered his subject, his vision. Hence the prominence he has given it, for instance also in his *Selected Poems 1957–1967*, where it has pride of place as the first poem in the collection. ■

1.3 When I say that with 'The Thought-Fox' Hughes seems to have discovered his subject, I do not mean to say that this is simply a matter of finding out how effectively he could write about animals, although that is certainly part of what he has discovered with it. Only five out of the forty poems in his first book *The Hawk in the Rain* actually centre on animals as their subject, and the proportion does not increase much with *Lupercal* or *Wodwo*; but they do include many of the best poems in these collections, and moreover his most recent work, from the *Crow* series onwards, does still tend to revolve around the animal world, at least initially. Hughes has often been labelled an animal poet, especially by his detractors; a point to which ironic tribute has been given by Vernon Scannell in his poem 'Ruminant', about a cow whose ruminations almost seem to include 'contemplating/Composing a long poem about Ted Hughes'. But if many of his best poems have animals, fish or birds as their ostensible subjects, it is soon evident that for all the sympathetic clarity and intuitive force with which a particular beast is evoked, Hughes is ultimately more concerned with individual, human nature than with animal. As we have seen, to call 'The Thought-Fox' an animal poem is accurate but insufficient, and when Hughes calls it that, he is careful to place the word 'animal' between quotation marks. His interest in the fox, and what one can only call the foxiness of the fox, is there to serve a deeper interest in individual feeling and experience. This should not be very surprising, especially to anyone familiar with D. H. Lawrence's poetry or even his novella, *The Fox* (see A302, Unit 30),[2] in which the animal is clearly there, it exists as a sharply defined and felt reality in the narrative, but it is also a metaphor for something else, some quality in human nature which the writer seeks to define, and yet which eludes the familiar terms in which we describe character.

Let's turn to 'The Thought-Fox' once again, and ask what kind of human feelings it seems to refer to. To begin with, I get a feeling of loneliness, frustration, even despair from it, summed up in that blank observation: 'Through the window I see no star' – to put it crudely, no guiding light. But, at the same time, there is something curiously ambivalent about this feeling, for the opening 'moment' brings a 'forest' – a bizarre yoking together of the abstract and the concrete if you think about it – and in this imagined, dream-like forest, a vague 'something' is alive, as if waiting. It is

[2]The Open University (1973) A302 *The Nineteenth Century Novel and Its Legacy*, Unit 30 *D. H. Lawrence* The Open University Press.

all a little horrific. This 'something' emerges gradually, uncertainly, until it is a 'bold' body, 'an eye' (a central image in Hughes's work), which focuses what is happening until with that 'sudden sharp hot stink of fox', the dark interior of the head is filled, a climax with oddly unpleasant sensations. It is as if the imagination at work is a threatening power, an idea reinforced by this sense of one's head as the secret lair of a predatory animal. The window remains starless, emphasizing that this process is essentially inward and lonely.

1.4 Many of Hughes's poems operate like dreams, conjuring up the state of special awareness with which dreams make us familiar. In another animal poem in *The Hawk in the Rain*, 'The Jaguar', although the beast which is its principal subject is brought clearly enough before us, that clarity has a hallucinatory quality which relates the poem to some deeper, dream level of perception.

The Jaguar

The apes yawn and adore their fleas in the sun.
The parrots shriek as if they were on fire, or strut
Like cheap tarts to attract the stroller with the nut.
Fatigued with indolence, tiger and lion

Lie still as the sun. The boa-constrictor's coil
Is a fossil. Cage after cage seems empty, or
Stinks of sleepers from the breathing straw.
It might be painted on a nursery wall.

But who runs like the rest past these arrives
At a cage where the crowd stands, stares, mesmerized,
As a child at a dream, at a jaguar hurrying enraged
Through prison darkness after the drills of his eyes

On a short fierce fuse. Not in boredom—
The eye satisfied to be blind in fire,
By the bang of blood in the brain deaf the ear—
He spins from the bars, but there's no cage to him

More than to the visionary his cell:
His stride is wildernesses of freedom:
The world rolls under the long thrust of his heel.
Over the cage floor the horizons come.

Thus Hughes's predator hurries 'enraged/Through prison darkness' before a crowd (spectators like ourselves) 'mesmerized,/As a child at a dream'. A further poem you might look at from this first collection, 'The Horses' (reprinted in *Selected Poems 1957–1967*), focuses on the eruption of a dawn sun over the 'grey silent world' in which the horses stand mysterious and 'Megalith-still', the whole scene becoming like the 'fever of a dream' for the narrator. Again, in a later poem on horses (as D. H. Lawrence knew, powerfully suggestive creatures for hinting at subconscious forces), 'A Dream of Horses', Hughes resorts to dream to evoke the deeper feelings of strangeness and power which, he seems to be saying, lie awaiting resurrection within us. This latter poem, which first appeared in Hughes's collection *Lupercal*, was taken by the critic A. Alvarez to be sufficiently representative of the powerful, new 'modern' poetry heralded in his anthology, *The New Poetry*, for him to contrast it with Philip Larkin's less urgent but gentler 'At Grass', suggesting that with the Hughes poem we delve much more deeply into ourselves. (You might like to make the comparison for yourself – both poems are quoted in full in Alvarez's introduction to his anthology, which is on your recommended reading list.) Subsequently, in *Wodwo* and in *Crow*, Hughes's dream turns to nightmare, as in his 'Ghost Crabs', which reveals blind, fearsome, yet oddly grotesque and even comic forces lumbering in a 'slow mineral fury' through us as we lie asleep, barely ruffled by the dim consciousness of what is happening within and around us. 'In our brains are many mansions, and most of the doors are locked, with the keys inside.' (Hughes *Poetry in the Making*, p 121.)

To anticipate a bit, here is 'Ghost Crabs' from *Wodwo*:

Ghost Crabs

At nightfall, as the sea darkens,
A depth darkness thickens, mustering from the gulfs and the
    submarine badlands,
To the sea's edge. To begin with
It looks like rocks uncovering, mangling their pallor.
Gradually the labouring of the tide
Falls back from its productions,
Its power slips back from glistening nacelles, and they are crabs.
Giant crabs, under flat skulls, staring inland
Like a packed trench of helmets.
Ghosts, they are ghost-crabs.
They emerge
An invisible disgorging of the sea's cold
Over the man who strolls along the sands.
They spill inland, into the smoking purple
Of our woods and towns – a bristling surge
Of tall and staggering spectres
Gliding like shocks through water.
Our walls, our bodies, are no problem to them.
Their hungers are homing elsewhere.
We cannot see them or turn our minds from them.
Their bubbling mouths, their eyes
In a slow mineral fury
Press through our nothingness where we sprawl on our beds,
Or sit in our rooms. Our dreams are ruffled maybe.
Or we jerk awake to the world of our possessions
With a gasp, in a sweat burst, brains jamming blind
Into the bulb-light. Sometimes, for minutes, a sliding
Staring
Thickness of silence
Presses between us. These crabs own this world.
All night, around us or through us,
They stalk each other, they fasten on to each other,
They mount each other, they tear each other to pieces,
They utterly exhaust each other.
They are the powers of this world.
We are their bacteria,
Dying their lives and living their deaths.
At dawn, they sidle back under the sea's edge.
They are the turmoil of history, the convulsion
In the roots of blood, in the cycles of concurrence.
To them, our cluttered countries are empty battleground.
All day they recuperate under the sea.
Their singing is like a thin sea-wind flexing in the rocks of a headland,
Where only crabs listen.

They are God's only toys.

1.5 Hughes conceives of us as typically living in a state of alienation from our 'real' selves, muffled by sensible, everyday life from both the violence and the vitality which surges beneath. 'I have tried to suggest', he writes, 'how infinitely beyond our ordinary notions of what we know our real knowledge, the real facts for us, really is. And to live removed from this inner universe of experience is also to live removed from ourself, banished from ourself and real life.' (Hughes *Poetry in the Making*, pp 123–4.) This is by no means a new idea: Blake, too, tried to evoke the natural energies which, he felt, were being warped and hidden by our rational, social selves. In a poem like 'The Thought-Fox', Hughes discovers the strange otherness of the imagination, which acts as a power of vision, an 'eye' coming 'about its own business', independently of our volition, to penetrate the secret lairs of the mind. And a similar process is at work in 'Ghost Crabs'. As with the great Romantics, Nature may be his subject, but it is ultimately the human psyche which concerns him most, and increasingly the darker, post-Freudian aspect in which our predatory, even monstrous, selves steal about.

1.6 But there is an important sense in which 'The Thought-Fox' is *not* typical of Hughes's work. I may well have exaggerated its slightly horrific quality, and the sense of power and energy lurking in it; for it is, as I am sure you've found in reading it aloud, a rather quiet, delicate poem. In this it is to some extent untypical, although the first collection does include such poems as 'October Dawn', which is similarly light and spare in effect.

October Dawn

October is marigold, and yet
A glass half full of wine left out

To the dark heaven all night, by dawn
Has dreamed a premonition

Of ice across its eye as if
The ice-age had begun its heave.

The lawn overtrodden and strewn
From the night before, and the whistling green

Shrubbery are doomed. Ice
Has got its spearhead into place.

First a skin, delicately here
Restraining a ripple from the air;

Soon plate and rivet on pond and brook;
Then tons of chain and massive lock

To hold rivers. Then, sound by sight
Will Mammoth and Sabre-tooth celebrate

Reunion while a fist of cold
Squeezes the fire at the core of the world,

Squeezes the fire at the core of the heart,
And now it is about to start.

1.7 More typical, perhaps, is the Hughes of the title poem of the collection, 'The Hawk in the Rain', an undeniably loud and powerful piece, with an immediate, battering-ram impact. And Hughes seems at times to attack his own more timid and uncertain verse in, for example, 'Famous Poet', a blustering, strained, satiric complaint against the old 'monsters' of the past who are now mouse-like in demeanour, lacking the 'vital fire' that poetry needs, unable to recreate what he calls the 'old heroic bang'. Two related poems in *The Hawk in the Rain*, 'Egg-Head' and 'The Man Seeking

Experience Enquires His Way of a Drop of Water', broaden the attack to include anyone who avoids the testing extremes of feeling which Hughes seems to believe we need to face in ourselves. But telling us this in a loud voice is, of course, no substitute for making us feel it. And yet, the best of *The Hawk in the Rain* does make us feel it: the range of feeling and experience may be narrow, despite Hughes's attempts to vary his subject (see, for instance, 'Secretary', written in the Auden-Larkin mould of light verse about urban victims; 'September', which attempts to catch a lyrical moment of love; and the war poems, especially 'The Casualty', reprinted and discussed by A. E. Dyson in the article on Hughes included in your Course Reader);[3] but the feeling itself is persistently deep and forceful.

In fact, one could say that Hughes himself manages to concoct the 'old heroic bang' he laments in 'Famous Poet', a phrase doubly apt in that his 'bang' is partly derived from the strong rhythms of the old heroic verse form, our native Old English four-beat alliterative poetry. As with Gerard Manley Hopkins, the very modernity of Hughes's line, his interest in a stress-based poetry which holds itself together by means of internal alliteration and assonance rather than end rhyme and metrical pattern, is paradoxical in being derived from a long and ancient tradition of writing verse going back to oral literature. But Hughes is always interested in what he has referred to (in praising the native vitality of Shakespeare's language) as 'the poetic instincts of English dialect' (*A Choice of Shakespeare's Verse*, p 11); an interest which, I think, correlates with his more general interest in the strength of the primitive in art and life.

The immediate influence of Hopkins on Hughes's first collection has been noticed by critics, although usually without detailed instances (see Dyson in your Course Reader, p 424). Of course, like any poet of his stature and individuality, there is a strict limit to how far it is useful to discuss his work in terms of influences, and, moreover, he draws on a multitude of English as well as (particularly in the later work) Continental and American writers – not to mention his fascination more recently with the folk art of less familiar cultures. But the first line of 'The Thought-Fox' clearly echoes Hopkins: I have in mind the opening of a poem which should be familiar to you from Record 1 *Rhythms of Poetry* (OU 21) which accompanies this course, 'The Windhover'. It begins: 'I caught this morning morning's minion . . .' But more interesting yet than this is 'The Hawk in the Rain' itself, which owes a lot in conception and manner to Hopkins's poetry and, I suspect, to 'The Windhover' in particular. Indeed, it may be worth turning now to 'The Hawk in the Rain', but I would like you to look first at 'The Windhover', and read it closely before reading Hughes's poem.

The Windhover

To Christ our Lord

I caught this morning morning's minion, king-
  dom of daylight's dauphin, dapple-dawn-drawn Falcon, in his riding
 Of the rolling level underneath him steady air, and striding
High there, how he rung upon the rein of a wimpling wing
In his ecstasy! then off, off forth on swing,
  As a skate's heel sweeps smooth on a bow-bend: the hurl and gliding
  Rebuffed the big wind. My heart in hiding
Stirred for a bird,—the achieve of, the mastery of the thing!

Brute beauty and valour and act, oh, air, pride, plume, here
  Buckle! AND the fire that breaks from thee then, a billion
 Times told lovelier, more dangerous, O my chevalier!

---

[3]Graham Martin and P. N. Furbank (eds.) (1975) *Twentieth Century Poetry: Critical Essays and Documents*, The Open University Press.

No wonder of it: shéer plód makes plough down sillion
Shine, and blue-bleak embers, ah my dear,
    Fall, gall themselves, and gash gold-vermilion.

The Hawk in the Rain

I drown in the drumming ploughland, I drag up
Heel after heel from the swallowing of the earth's mouth,
From clay that clutches my each step to the ankle
With the habit of the dogged grave, but the hawk

Effortlessly at height hangs his still eye.
His wings hold all creation in a weightless quiet,
Steady as a hallucination in the streaming air.
While banging wind kills these stubborn hedges,

Thumbs my eyes, throws my breath, tackles my heart,
And rain hacks my head to the bone, the hawk hangs
The diamond point of will that polestars
The sea drowner's endurance: and I,

Bloodily grabbed dazed last-moment-counting
Morsel in the earth's mouth, strain towards the master-
Fulcrum of violence where the hawk hangs still.
That maybe in his own time meets the weather

Coming the wrong way, suffers the air, hurled upside down,
Fall from his eye, the ponderous shires crash on him,
The horizon trap him; the round angelic eye
Smashed, mix his heart's blood with the mire of the land.

■   Now how does Hughes's poem compare with 'The Windhover'? Is it a similar kind of poem, or are there overriding differences?

Discussion

1.8   'The Windhover' is, I believe, a useful starting point here, because it serves as a reminder that, although when the poems in *The Hawk in the Rain* first came out, they hit the English poetic scene like a bombshell, this was in some ways more the product of the prevailing trend towards self-effacing, detached, and above all *safe* verse, than the result of Hughes's own striking originality. On its appearance, Edwin Muir called Hughes's collection 'A most surprising first book', remarking that the poet seemed to be 'quite outside the currents of his time'.[4] He was. And yet he was also turning back towards the verbal richness, the daring rhetoric, the experimentalism of Yeats, D. H. Lawrence, Dylan Thomas and, before them, Hopkins.[5] The reaction against 'modernism' which dominated some of the most influential poetry being written in the 1950s passed him by. This much can be seen in 'The Hawk in the Rain'. Like 'The Windhover', what we have here is a magnificent, breathtaking enactment of the power and energy of a bird. Like Hopkins, Hughes hammers the reader with his emphatic rhythms and strongly marked stresses ('I drown in the

[4] *New Statesman*, 20 September 1957.
[5] Note that the poems of Hopkins (in my view an unfortunate gap in A306), though published by Robert Bridges in 1918, had no appreciable effect on English poetry until two decades or more later; Hopkins was a 'modernist' before his time.

drumming ploughland, I drag up'), violent verbs ('Thumbs my eyes, throws my breath, tackles my heart'), huge adjectival phrases ('Bloodily grabbed dazed last-moment-counting') and a free use of run-on lines – all to evoke the striving and ecstasy of the state of being which is identified with the hawk or, in Hopkins's case, the kestrel. (You might also like to compare 'The Hawk in the Rain' with another and perhaps nearer source, Dylan Thomas's 'Over Sir John's Hill', which Walford Davies analyses at the end of Unit 26.)

Hopkins identifies the bird's state of being with Christ: grace of movement becomes divine grace. And in a sense, Hughes's poem is also religious in feeling, although not specifically Christian: he evokes awe for the possibility of perfect power and mastery in nature which can transcend itself (the bird meets the weather coming to smash him 'maybe in his own time') to the point of defeating death. Both poems exploit a dualism between matter and spirit: matter as the earth, where mortality, death resides; the spirit as the height of the sky which seems to hold out hope of escape into timelessness. Compare Hopkins's image of himself as a 'heart' in 'hiding' down where 'shéer plód makes plough down sillion/Shine' ('sillion' means furrow), but stirred by the high striding above him of the 'Falcon, in his riding/Of the rolling underneath him steady air'; compare this with Hughes's narrator clutched by the clay of the earth like a 'dogged grave', yet aware of the hawk who – and the word 'hawk' is brilliantly suspended at the end of the line to mimic this – 'Effortlessly at height hangs his still eye.' For Hughes, the sky is closed, the horizon is a trap; in other words, death brings no redemptive hope. But for Hopkins, the fall of the bird to earth is conceived as a kind of splendid triumph, invoking the Christian paradox of the fall of man: thus the 'gash gold-vermilion', the bright new colours revealed by slicing into earth. For him, resurrection is possible. But the most that is suggested by 'The Hawk in the Rain' is that you can choose when to die, and yet even as the hawk seems effortlessly 'still' (a word which holds the meanings of both calmness and eternity), and beyond the deathly clutches of the earth, we realize it is deluded, or part of a delusion: the ambiguity of 'hallucination' prepares us for the last stanza, in which it is shown to be only subjectively that death can be met 'in his own time', for the bird is smashed to mere blood and mire. What is important is the will, that 'diamond point' of indestructibility which directs as the polestar to a sea drowner (a metaphor somewhat arbitrarily brought into the poem, in terms of its progression of images focusing man's endurance, his will to survive).

This will to survive, a kind of unflinching stoicism in the face of the arbitrary violence of death, is a major theme in Ted Hughes's work, and it often emerges, as here, from the tension of opposing forces, a conflict of matter and spirit resolved only temporarily in that taut balance of the 'master-/Fulcrum of violence'. Violence itself is the lesser theme: it is a form of uncontrolled energy which may give life or destroy it, depending on the nature of its appearance. In both 'The Windhover' and 'The Hawk in the Rain', we are shown that it is a vision, a way of seeing (Hughes concentrates again on the eye, finally a 'round angelic eye'), which determines whether one is vitally alive or as good as dead. To me, this is the deep level of closeness between Hughes and Hopkins, beyond the closeness of language and device which we have already seen. Yet again, there are essential differences in their fundamental views and perceptions, evident in these poems: Hopkins has the confidence of his concluding consolation, a confidence reflected too in his ultimately more traditional, stricter form: 'The Windhover' is a sonnet, whereas Hughes's poem is written in an unrhymed, looser stanza-pattern. Moreover, Hughes reveals a kind of desperation in the face of his own awareness of death which leads to a rhetoric of exaggeration which eventually becomes numbing, overwhelming one's initial responsiveness to all his driving energy and sensuality of expression (how can rain really hack one's head to the bone?). This may indeed be why the poem has been excluded from his *Selected Poems*. ■

2 LUPERCAL

2.1 Hughes's first collection of poems was criticized on its appearance (and has been since) for being derivative and excessively interested in violence. As I've tried to suggest, there are decipherable influences, such as Hopkins, but these do not necessarily detract from the quality of the poetry; nor is the poetry obsessively interested in violence as such. Hughes himself has written: 'My poems are not about violence but vitality' (in an interview in the *Guardian*, 23 March 1965). And if physical action is emphasized much more in his work than in a comparable poet such as Hopkins, it is because for Hughes the sheer vitality of primal nature, in animal and man, has had to take over the place of God in the universe. 'Any form of violence – any form of vehement activity – invokes the bigger energy, the elemental power circuit of the Universe.' (Faas 'Ted Hughes and Crow' *London Magazine*, new series X, p 9.)

The problem is how to control this energy, and this, according to Hughes, is done by means of rituals, 'the machinery of religion'. In a post-Christian age, or one at least in which Christianity is disintegrating, other myths must be created, or rediscovered. Thus for Hughes, violence *is* seen in a human context, a cultural context; and this is something which is often missed by readers of his work.

2.2 Perhaps the poem which has created the most misunderstanding, but which is also one of his finest, is 'Hawk Roosting', from *Lupercal*, the collection of poems which appeared in March 1960, after Ted and Sylvia Hughes had been living in the United States for some three years. This poem above all established Hughes's reputation – and notoriety, in some circles. What do *you* think of it?

Hawk Roosting

I sit in the top of the wood, my eyes closed.
Inaction, no falsifying dream
Between my hooked head and hooked feet:
Or in sleep rehearse perfect kills and eat.

The convenience of the high trees!
The air's buoyancy and the sun's ray
Are of advantage to me;
And the earth's face upward for my inspection.

My feet are locked upon the rough bark.
It took the whole of Creation
To produce my foot, my each feather:
Now I hold Creation in my foot

Or fly up, and revolve it all slowly—
I kill where I please because it is all mine.
There is no sophistry in my body:
My manners are tearing off heads—

The allotment of death.
For the one path of my flight is direct
Through the bones of the living.
No arguments assert my right:

The sun is behind me.
Nothing has changed since I began.
My eye has permitted no change.
I am going to keep things like this.

■ What is Hughes's attitude towards his subject? Has it changed from 'The Hawk in the Rain'? Has the *style* changed?

Discussion

2.3 I think one's first impression, especially after reading 'The Hawk in the Rain', is of *controlled* violence, reflected in Hughes's shift to a new economy and brevity of utterance. Gone is the sledgehammer rhetoric of the earlier poem; gone, too, are the echoes of Hopkins. As we have seen, some of the earlier poetry – 'The Thought-Fox', for example, or 'October Dawn' – shows the delicacy and control Hughes is capable of; but there is an austerity about this, and a consistency with which the initial idea is developed, which heralds a maturer poet, someone more confident in his own abilities and vision.

Hughes's attitude has changed. This poem is, of course, a monologue, told from the point of view of a hawk sitting in the top of a wood. Unlike 'The Hawk in the Rain', no distinction is drawn between the observing, human intelligence and the creature observed. But what is it all about?

The hawk is apparently in a solipsistic trance, self-admiring and single-minded in the pursuit of its end, which is the 'allotment of death'. He says there is 'no sophistry in my body', no 'arguments' to 'assert my right'. This develops and emphasizes the opening idea that 'no falsifying dream' comes between the hawk's hooked head and hooked feet, reminding us, by contrast, of man, who is limited by the 'dream' of consciousness, which separates him from the beasts. Unlike the sense of dream in 'The Jaguar' or 'A Dream of Horses', here 'dream' suggests thought, ratiocination, the process that as it were interferes to distort the connection between impulse and action. In the words of Brutus, contemplating the death of Caesar: 'Between the acting of a dreadful thing/And the first motion, all the interim is/Like a phantasma, or a hideous dream' (*Julius Caesar*, II i 63–5). But that dream is conscience: to put it aside is to try and become like an animal, without guilt or shame, for consciousness also involves a moral sense.

Thus the hawk's function defines its being; and the poem apparently reveals it glorying in what it is. The question is, does Hughes glory in what it is, too? Critics have taken this as the essential meaning of the poem, extending it to include a glorification of fascism, although the poem avoids specifying overtly the social or historical aspects of its subject. You will have to decide for yourself whether or not the poem can be used in this way, or to what extent the charge is true. My own feeling, as you will guess from what I've already said about the exaggerated place that has been given to violence as a central theme in Hughes's work, is that it is a misreading of the poem to take it to be glorifying the hawk's point of view. There *are* poems by Hughes, especially some of his weaker ones (the weaker ones tend to get used to support the case that Hughes celebrates mindless violence), which imply a rather crude worship of big-chested brutality – for instance, 'The Ancient Heroes and the Bomber Pilot' in *The Hawk in the Rain*. But in 'Hawk Roosting', it seems to me, what we have is essentially a further development of the view suggested in the earlier hawk poem; namely, that the bird is subject to a delusion, a delusion which is attractive, and by which we may wish to live, but a delusion nonetheless.

If this view seems puzzling, you may like to look at the poem again. In particular, at the last line. What impact does it have on your feelings about the poem as a whole? To me, the effect is similar to the double-take one experiences at the conclusion of 'The Thought-Fox': a moment of dramatic revelation, especially if you read it aloud. 'I am going to keep things like this.' The line can only be read ironically, I feel. By this stage, there is something ludicrous about the huge pretensions of the hawk, its belief not only that the high trees, the air's buoyancy, the sun, the earth, are there for its convenience, but also, with sublime egoism, that the whole purpose of Creation was to produce its foot, each individual feather. Moreover, reading the surprisingly short sentences which make up the poem – the syntax of manic certitude – until, in the last stanza, we have four lines each made up of a complete sentence, confirms one's realization of what the poem ultimately presents: a vision of the complete insanity of power.

The hawk thinks it has the power of God: it can hold that whole Creation which went into its making. In *Crow*, God is shown to labour under the same delusion. Here, there are social, historical implications, confirmed by Hughes's remark elsewhere that the hawk sounds 'like Hitler's familiar spirit'. (Faas 'Ted Hughes and Crow' p 8.) If the social or historical dimension seems to be omitted from Hughes's work, this is not because the poet is unaware of it; rather, he goes straight to what seem to him to be the deeper undercurrents, and he does so in such a way that we are brought to *share* the delusion without the detachment possible where everything is spelled out in more overt detail. As Michael Hamburger has written, in the line 'My manners are tearing off heads –', the single word 'manners' is enough to make the connection between the ferocious ways of this predator and the ways of mankind. (Hamburger *The Truth of Poetry*, p 310.) ∎

2.4 Other poems in *Lupercal* are more explicit about the human implications of the violence or, as Hughes would prefer to call it, the *energy* he perceives in animal nature. 'Pike' is the most brilliant example of this, although you should look also at 'The Bull Moses', 'View of a Pig', and, among the poems not specifically dealing with animals, 'Mayday in Holderness', 'Relic' (reprinted in Press, *A Map of Modern English Verse*, p 265), and 'November'. In this last poem, Hughes, who sometimes shows a Wordsworthian interest in wandering outcasts, observes a tramp 'bundled asleep' in a ditch under the 'drilling rain', apparently dead, but in fact surviving through an animal-like, even elemental (he is compared to a hedgehog, then a stone) clinging to existence. Throughout these poems, though usually more obliquely, the poet is concerned to express this sense of life on the edge of existence, threatened by the vast darkness of death. Here is 'November':

November

The month of the drowned dog. After long rain the land
Was sodden as the bed of an ancient lake,
Treed with iron and birdless. In the sunk lane
The ditch – a seep silent all summer –

Made brown foam with a big voice: that, and my boots
On the lane's scrubbed stones, in the gulleyed leaves,
Against the hill's hanging silence;
Mist silvering the droplets on the bare thorns

Slower than the change of daylight.
In a let of the ditch a tramp was bundled asleep:
Face tucked down into beard, drawn in
Under its hair like a hedgehog's. I took him for dead,

But his stillness separated from the death
Of the rotting grass and the ground. A wind chilled,
And a fresh comfort tightened through him,
Each hand stuffed deeper into the other sleeve.

His ankles, bound with sacking and hairy band,
Rubbed each other, resettling. The wind hardened;
A puff shook a glittering from the thorns,
And again the rains' dragging grey columns

Smudged the farms. In a moment
The fields were jumping and smoking; the thorns
Quivered, riddled with the glassy verticals.
I stayed on under the welding cold

Watching the tramp's face glisten and the drops on his coat
Flash and darken. I thought what strong trust
Slept in him – as the trickling furrows slept,
And the thorn-roots in their grip on darkness;

And the buried stones, taking the weight of winter;
The hill where the hare crouched with clenched teeth.
Rain plastered the land till it was shining
Like hammered lead, and I ran, and in the rushing wood

Shuttered by a black oak leaned.
The keeper's gibbet had owls and hawks
By the neck, weasels, a gang of cats, crows:
Some, stiff, weightless, twirled like dry bark bits

In the drilling rain. Some still had their shape,
Had their pride with it; hung, chins on chests,
Patient to outwait these worst days that beat
Their crowns bare and dripped from their feet.

2.5   If Hughes explores 'extreme' emotions in his poetry, he does so under the pressure of a vision which is constantly aware of the massive ebb and flow of natural forces underlying all life. With some important exceptions, he expresses this vision most successfully when dealing with the non-human world, at least on the surface, allowing the human implications to trickle in secretly, of their own accord. In a poem such as 'Thrushes', after a startlingly effective opening which perceives the birds as similar to the hawk of 'Hawk Roosting' in their terrifyingly efficient, single-minded 'bounce and stab' in pursuit of their purpose, he is unfortunately tempted to try reflecting upon these implications more directly, with clumsy results. Do you see what I mean?

Thrushes

Terrifying are the attent sleek thrushes on the lawn,
More coiled steel than living – a poised
Dark deadly eye, those delicate legs
Triggered to stirrings beyond sense – with a start, a bounce, a stab
Overtake the instant and drag out some writhing thing.
No indolent procrastinations and no yawning stares,
No sighs or head-scratchings. Nothing but bounce and stab
And a ravening second.

Is it their single-mind-sized skulls, or a trained
Body, or genius, or a nestful of brats
Gives their days this bullet and automatic
Purpose? Mozart's brain had it, and the shark's mouth
That hungers down the blood-smell even to a leak of its own
Side and devouring of itself: efficiency which
Strikes too streamlined for any doubt to pluck at it
Or obstruction deflect.

With a man it is otherwise. Heroisms on horseback,
Outstripping his desk-diary at a broad desk,
Carving at a tiny ivory ornament
For years: his act worships itself – while for him,
Though he bends to be blent in the prayer, how loud and above what
Furious spaces of fire do the distracting devils
Orgy and hosannah, under what wilderness
Of black silent waters weep.

The murderous suddenness with which impulse translates into act in the thrushes
is compared with 'Mozart's brain', and 'the shark's mouth/That hungers down the
blood-smell even to a leak of its own/Side and devouring of itself', an arbitrary
yoking together of associations which lacks the persuasive inevitability of 'Hawk
Roosting'. Moreover, the last three lines seem to me fine-sounding but empty
gestures towards the powers Hughes pretends to tell us live outside the little world of
our desk-diary lives. To my mind, there is a failure of intuition here.

2.6 In 'Pike', the human, even personal (the poem has a distinctly autobiographical
feel), is allowed in by a masterful shifting of perspectives, starting with the familiar
Hughes identification with the creature which names the poem, through a domestic
vista of the fish as a grotesque pet, and on to a remembered experience which
gradually deepens into a final nightmare perception of horror and mystery at
the heart of things. To read this poem is to recognize how it is that Hughes has
become one of the most praised English poets of his generation.

Pike

Pike, three inches long, perfect
Pike in all parts, green tigering the gold.
Killers from the egg: the malevolent aged grin.
They dance on the surface among the flies.

Or move, stunned by their own grandeur,
Over a bed of emerald, silhouette
Of submarine delicacy and horror.
A hundred feet long in their world.

In ponds, under the heat-struck lily pads –
Gloom of their stillness:
Logged on last year's black leaves, watching upwards.
Or hung in an amber cavern of weeds

The jaws' hooked clamp and fangs
Not to be changed at this date;
A life subdued to its instrument;
The gills kneading quietly, and the pectorals.

Three we kept behind glass,
Jungled in weed: three inches, four,
And four and a half: fed fry to them –
Suddenly there were two. Finally one

With a sag belly, and the grin it was born with.
And indeed they spare nobody.
Two, six pounds each, over two feet long,
High and dry and dead in the willow-herb –

Figure 2 Breughel the Elder Big Fish Eat Little Fish, *1556, pencil drawing* (Graphische Sammlung Albertina, Vienna)

One jammed past its gills down the other's gullet:
The outside eye stared: as a vice locks –
The same iron in this eye
Though its film shrank in death.

A pond I fished, fifty yards across,
Whose lilies and muscular tench
Had outlasted every visible stone
Of the monastery that planted them –

Stilled legendary depth:
It was as deep as England. It held
Pike too immense to stir, so immense and old
That past nightfall I dared not cast

But silently cast and fished
With the hair frozen on my head
For what might move, for what eye might move.
The still splashes on the dark pond,

Owls hushing the floating woods
Frail on my ear against the dream
Darkness beneath night's darkness had freed,
That rose slowly towards me, watching.

2.7 Some aspects of this remarkable poem should be familiar by now as lasting features of Ted Hughes's work: the opening sensual impression of the fearful perfection of nature in its destructiveness; the rich, densely powerful imagery unfolding with progressive inevitability as the poem's meanings ripple outwards; the strong, insistent, stress-based rhythms reinforcing this onward movement, yet carefully restrained by the four-line stanzas which provide a balance and structure for the whole. As in his preceding poems, Hughes binds the verses tightly together by means of internal rhyme, alliteration and assonance, concentrating especially on hard, plosive consonants to add to the effect of suddenness and harshness in the phenomena evoked – 'Pike in all parts, green tigering the gold./Killers from the egg: the malevolent aged grin.' By contrast with the brevity and even violence with which one is encouraged to utter 'Pike', 'parts', 'egg' and 'grin', the drawn-out words 'tigering' and 'malevolent' let the reader linger over their implications, so that the fish's 'dance' becomes a macabre celebration of timeless, instinctive evil. And this kind of effect continues throughout the poem, evoking sharp impressions of the immediate impact of the creature, at the same time stirring up atavistic memories of the primitive horrors rising towards the surface of consciousness in the narrator.

Interestingly, 'Pike' *has* a narrator, first introduced in the fifth stanza ('Three we kept behind glass'), apparently as a child or young member of a household – 'Jungled' evokes a boy's impression of a fish tank, at the same time adding a new and limiting perspective to the opening impressions of 'submarine delicacy and horror'; and this narrator goes on to give further new dimensions to the poem as it continues, quietly measuring the fish as if to contain them that way, but unable to avoid the memory of two of 'six pounds each', dead in the willow-herb (a nicely English domestic rural touch), jammed into each other in the merciless cannibalism of the species. Then, in what is evidently the final, third section of this carefully structured poem (the stanzas fall into the arrangement 4–3–4), the narrator, now 'I', still struggling to resist the full impact of his own impressions by noting prosaic details such as that the pond he fished is 'fifty yards across', is forced to confront the reality which, like an 'eye', a 'dream' (familiar images) comes towards him. The 'legendary depth', as 'deep as England', in which the nameless horror has its being, seems to imply an historical perspective too, and suggests that in our own cosy corner of civilization, with its quiet, domestic surface, there survive primitive forces whose evil otherness can only be dimly hinted at, but which – in the most disturbing aspect of the poem's meaning – are watching, waiting.

There is much more to be said about 'Pike', but I have tried to suggest a little of what seems to me to be important about it. To some extent, I have stressed the formal qualities it reveals, and the way in which it seems to represent a continuation of Hughes's earlier techniques and obsessions. The reason for this is that *Lupercal* can be seen as bringing to an end a phase in the poet's work. Fittingly, perhaps, the concluding image of the book, from the title-poem, 'Lupercalia', begs:

> Maker of the world,
> Hurrying the lit ghost of man
> Age to age while the body hold,
> Touch this frozen one.[6]

But the divine energies of creativity he is pleading after do not touch him, they remain at a distance until, years later, they re-emerge in a new book, *Wodwo*.

[6]The Lupercalia were Roman rituals celebrated on 15 February for the purpose of restoring fertility to barren women, who were struck with whips by athletes racing through the streets; Lupercas was associated with Pan and Dionysus, deities of prodigality and generation.

3 WODWO

3.1 Ted Hughes and Sylvia Plath returned to England shortly before the publication of *Lupercal* to settle permanently. Initially in London, they moved to Devon and a thatched cottage where Hughes still lives. Their children, Frieda and Nicholas, were born in 1960 and 1962. Sylvia Plath wrote her autobiographical novel, *The Bell Jar*, and some of the poems to be later published in *Ariel*. Hughes himself continued to write, but it was to be seven years after *Lupercal* before he published his next collection of poems for adults and for general distribution – *Wodwo*, which appeared in May 1967. In the intervening years his creativity flickered fitfully, in poems and stories for children, such as *The Earth Owl and Other Moon People* (1963: verse), or *Nessie the Mannerless Monster* (1963: prose), as well as in some rather fugitive pieces brought out as a volume of poems in a limited edition, *Recklings* (1966). Some of these 'recklings' (i.e. runts, the weakest of a litter), which represented experiments in a new, stripped but private style, were permitted to survive: 'Logos' in the English edition of *Wodwo*, and several others in the American edition, including 'Root, Stem, Leaf', which was also retained for the *Selected Poems*. During the years between Sylvia Plath's suicide in 1963, and the appearance of *Recklings*, Hughes wrote little or nothing.

3.2 *Wodwo*, the author told his readers in a prefatory note, should be read as a single work, including not only the poems which make up Parts I and III, but the five short stories and the play in Part II. This was wishful thinking: the life, originality and force of the volume are in the poetry rather than in the sub-Lawrentian tales or the nightmare play it contains. Yet the different pieces do expose the essentially experimental, exploratory quality of *Wodwo*: Hughes is daring to take entirely new turns to try and express his vision. In retrospect, he looks to be fumbling, and even at the time *Wodwo* appeared, it did not elicit much enthusiasm from reviewers and critics; yet, as the title poem alone indicated, Hughes was making striking poetry out of his struggle towards new forms. The essentially modern desire to penetrate further into himself and his experience was driving him into a new experimentation, an experimentation which was to lead in the end to the remarkable *Crow* poems, radically different in style if not in subject from the earlier work.

3.3 It is worth turning immediately to the title poem, 'Wodwo', with which Hughes concluded his volume, summing this collection up while promising to 'go on looking'. A 'wodwo', I should mention, is itself a mystery word, derived from the fourteenth-century alliterative epic romance, *Sir Gawain and the Green Knight*, in which it is used apparently (although no one can be sure) to describe a wild, half-human, half-animal creature met with in lonely places by the hero, Sir Gawain. Its aptness will be immediately apparent to you.

> *Wodwo*
>
> What am I? Nosing here, turning leaves over
> Following a faint stain on the air to the river's edge
> I enter water. What am I to split
> The glassy grain of water looking upward I see the bed
> Of the river above me upside down very clear
> What am I doing here in mid-air? Why do I find
> this frog so interesting as I inspect its most secret
> interior and make it my own? Do these weeds
> know me and name me to each other have they
> seen me before, do I fit in their world? I seem
> separate from the ground and not rooted but dropped
> out of nothing casually I've no threads
> fastening me to anything I can go anywhere

I seem to have been given the freedom
of this place what am I then? And picking
bits of bark off this rotten stump gives me
no pleasure and it's no use so why do I do it
me and doing that have coincided very queerly
But what shall I be called am I the first
have I an owner what shape am I what
shape am I am I huge if I go
to the end on this way past these trees and past these trees
till I get tired that's touching one wall of me
for the moment if I sit still how everything
stops to watch me I suppose I am the exact centre
but there's all this what is it roots
roots roots roots and here's the water
again very queer but I'll go on looking

■   Now how does this splendid poem compare with Hughes's earlier verse? To
what extent have the manner and the matter changed?

Discussion

3.4   This is surely a delightfully funny poem, a sardonic little Yorkshire comedy, including, perhaps, the poet himself as a physical presence – 'am I huge' – Hughes
is in fact an immense man, and was not surprisingly mistaken for a security guard
when on a poetry reading tour in Israel. Perhaps the most obvious point about the
poem is that what we have here is a gentle, humorous portrait of a beast, with none
of the urgency or terror created by the earlier poems such as 'The Hawk in the
Rain' or 'Hawk Roosting'. This is once again a monologue, told from the point
of view of the creature which is its subject (compare 'Hawk Roosting'), but as the
questing beast starts off by asking 'What am I?' and, indeed, as the whole point of
the poem seems to be that we are left uncertain about the nature of the creature,
and even whether or not it is human like the poet or animal like his earlier creations,
to call it simply a monologue seems ludicrously inappropriate. Hughes is, in fact,
moving away from the world of conventional poetic terminology here. More than
this, he is moving away from the world of language conventions as well. Thus,
you will notice that whereas in all the poems we have dealt with so far, Hughes
has maintained the conventions of syntax, and punctuation, even when he has
been at his most elliptical, as in, say, 'Pike', here he begins to drop even those
conventions. And just as in so many of the earlier poems the way the poem is written
acts out the sense of the poem so, here, to begin with, he uses at least some of the
conventions of syntax and punctuation, but as the poem proceeds, you can see that
even the commas and full stops and question marks disappear, as the language
becomes more questionable and uncertain, until finally even the capital letters at
the beginnings of lines or sentences are lost, and we are left with

have I an owner what shape am I what
shape am I am I huge if I go
to the end on this way past these trees and past these trees

and so on to the end. Hughes's earlier verse could be called 'free', but compared
to this, it is only 'half-free', being still subject to conventions of rhyme, stanza
pattern, clearly-marked stress rhythms and syntax. Here Hughes breaks into the
much freer form of the Americans such as Olson or Carlos Williams, or, one might

add, of their forebears among the 'modernist' movement, such as T. S. Eliot. Of course, the verse is still evidently subject to controls or limits, implicit in the ordering of the words on the page and in the subtle undercurrents of rhythm, emphasized by alliteration and assonance as in 'till I get tired that's touching one wall of me'. Simple repetition becomes more important, and the movement of the 'wodwo' is recreated by such means as the repetition of 'past these trees' in the lines above, as well as by ironic reiteration in 'but there's all this what is it roots/roots roots roots', giving the feel of a creature rooting about – for its roots.

Hughes questions himself in this poem, and he questions the kind of poetry he writes: 'Why do I find/this frog so interesting as I inspect its most secret/interior and make it my own?' The self-assurance out of which, in the earlier poems, Hughes made animals his own, has become corroded, so that what he has to do now, all he *can* do now, is continue to explore the 'very queer' nature of reality, and 'go on looking'. ■

4 CROW

4.1 Thus, after *Wodwo*, Hughes's treatment of the animal world, his ostensible major subject all along, becomes radically different. It has been freed from almost all ties to the actual attributes of the animals evoked. Yet, in a sense, isn't this really a continuation of the position he established right at the start? The 'Thought-Fox' was never just a fox. And in the so-called 'Crow' poems, the first of which began to appear in 1967, and which were collected into *Crow: From the Life and Songs of the Crow* in 1970, Hughes goes a step further: the real attributes of his creature take on a surreal, mythical dimension. Everyday reality seems to have become even more suspect than it appeared in *Wodwo*. The conventions of language become as questionable as the nature of the experience which language tries to shape and communicate. These new poems appear in an original, bare and fragmentary dialect – yet one composed of the scraps of folklore, myth and religion which formerly provided man with an explanation of himself and his world, and so one riddled with associations from the past. Hughes has said that

> The first idea of *Crow* was really an idea of a style. In folktales the prince going on the adventure comes to the stable full of beautiful horses and he needs a horse for the next stage and the king's daughter advises him to take none of the beautiful horses that he'll be offered but to choose the dirty, scabby little foal. You see, I throw out the eagles and choose the Crow. The idea was originally just to write his songs, the songs that a Crow would sing. In other words, songs with no music whatsoever, in a super-simple and super-ugly language which would in a way shed everything except just what he wanted to say without any other consideration and that's the basis of the style of the whole thing. I get near it in a few poems. There I really begin to get near what I was after. (Faas 'Ted Hughes and Crow', p 20.)

4.2 A crow is an intelligent, widely distributed and omnivorous bird, black, solitary, tough and unmusical; as an eater of carrion, it is dependent on death and destruction, and is a kind of digestive machine in flight. All these attributes are present in Hughes's bird, but they are subordinated by the apocalyptic context in which it turns up in the cycle or series (originally intended to be an epic folk tale in prose with the

Crow songs interspersed, a project perhaps fortunately unlikely to be completed, as Hughes's ventures into fictional prose or drama have not been very happy). The prime source of these contexts is Christianity, in particular the familiar Biblical account of the history of the world and man's place in it, from beginning to end. Hughes anticipated this in one or two poems in *Wodwo*, for instance 'Theology':

Theology

No, the serpent did not
Seduce Eve to the apple.
All that's simply
Corruption of the facts.

Adam ate the apple.
Eve ate Adam.
The serpent ate Eve.
This is the dark intestine.

The serpent, meanwhile,
Sleeps his meal off in Paradise –
Smiling to hear
God's querulous calling.

4.3 This humorous and startling reversal of the Fall, with its emphasis upon digestion ('This is the dark intestine') and God's ineffectiveness, is characteristic of the 'Crow' poems. Yet in *Crow*, what we have is much more powerful, frightening and painful, as well as comic, and this is primarily because of the unifying presence of the Crow itself, which is fundamentally a metaphor, like Hughes's 'Thought-Fox', but one extended by its use in so many different contexts so that it becomes mythical. Here is one example of how it appears, in a new account of the Fall:

A Childish Prank

Man's and woman's bodies lay without souls,
Dully gaping, foolishly staring, inert
On the flowers of Eden.
God pondered.

The problem was so great, it dragged him asleep.

Crow laughed.
He bit the Worm, God's only son,
Into two writhing halves.

He stuffed into man the tail half
With the wounded end hanging out.

He stuffed the head half headfirst into woman
And it crept in deeper and up
To peer out through her eyes
Calling its tail-half to join up quickly, quickly
Because O it was painful.

Man awoke being dragged across the grass.
Woman awoke to see him coming.
Neither knew what had happened.

God went on sleeping.

Crow went on laughing.

26

4.4 Thus the mischievous Crow exists in a kind of nightmare which paradoxically reveals to us the truth which God omits to tell us – that is, the outmoded, 'sleeping' God of the Christian myth. The grisly humour of much of the poems about Crow, a combination of the gruesome and the horrific, relates Hughes less to any recognizable English or even American poet, than to the Eastern Europeans such as Zbigniev Herbert and Vasko Popa, poets you will be looking at later in this course. Some of Popa's surreal little allegories, 'The Donkey', 'Starry Snail' and 'The Story of a Story', are included in Hughes's *Poetry in the Making*. Hughes also wrote a revealing – more revealing about himself than about Popa – introduction to Popa's *Selected Poems* (1969).

4.5 Popa, says Hughes, writes in the knowledge that man's politics have been 'weighed out in dead bodies by the million', and yet that man is also 'at the same time and in the same circumstances, an acutely conscious human creature of suffering and hope' with, perhaps, 'doubtful and provisional senses, so undefinable as to be almost silly, but palpably existing, and wanting to go on existing'. To express this vision, Popa, like Hughes, who writes in the same knowledge, creates a 'small, ironic space' with his short, grisly but playful lyrics, a space in the surrounding darkness of nihilism. In Popa we have the 'surrealism of folklore', a down-to-earth, primitive but practical form of discourse, made up of cycles of poems on a given theme, each creating the terms of its own little universe. The 'little fable of visionary anecdote' is the basis of this kind of poetry, as it is of Hughes's. (Popa *Selected Poems*, pp 9–12.)

5 CONCLUSION

5.1 I cannot really 'sum up' here, for, as you will have gathered from my opening remarks, I believe that only provisional judgements can be made at this stage about a poet still active as Hughes is. And I have limited my discussion of *Crow*, leaving it to you to pursue Hughes further into that world of startling absurdities and intense experiences if you have felt an interest in what you have so far read of Hughes's work.

5.2 But perhaps I should try to draw some threads together, at least. What I think may be seen in Hughes's development from *The Hawk in the Rain* to *Crow* is essentially an expansion of the unique force and intensity of the earliest poems, such as 'The Hawk in the Rain', or 'The Jaguar', through 'Hawk Roosting' and 'Pike' (the supreme poems of this time), and continued in 'Ghost Crabs', until in the 'Crow' cycle a more symbolic and fragmentary form of verse appears to take over, in which the subtleties and fine nuances of feeling and expression, present in, say, 'The Thought-Fox' or 'October Dawn' or even 'Wodwo', are sacrificed to a further intensification of power and *energy*. At the same time, Hughes has shown himself, despite his links with the poetry of the Romantics (even *Crow* is suggestive of, say, some of Blake's prophetic verse), to be a firmly 'modernist' writer, in the sense of a writer who, like Eliot and Pound, and unlike Hardy, sees his age as an age of crisis, of decay in the moral and religious myths of the European tradition, and thus is concerned to express and clarify his own vision in an attempt to redefine what is necessary for minimal human survival. He goes beyond the earlier 'modernists' in his awareness that a mere reordering and redefining of the older European tradition is not enough; but then he is operating in an age when the word 'incinerate' (which turns up obsessively in *Crow*), has become horribly familiar, and when cultural tinkering cannot bring salvation. In short, Hughes's vision is an apocalyptic vision, he inevitably ends by invoking the myths of creation and destruction, life and death.

Yet in Hughes's end lies his beginning, as I have tried to suggest. It may be no surprise to learn that as early as September 1957, on the occasion of the selection of *The Hawk in the Rain* as the Poetry Book Society's Autumn Choice, Hughes announced in the Society's Bulletin that: 'What excites my imagination is the war between vitality and death.' It is his final theme.

SUGGESTIONS FOR FURTHER WORK ON TED HUGHES

1   As Roger Day suggests in Unit 28, *Philip Larkin*, you may like to compare Hughes and Larkin as poets. A useful starting-point might be A. Alvarez's introduction to *The New Poetry* (Penguin, 1962), in which the comparison is made between Larkin's 'At Grass' and Hughes's 'A Dream of Horses'. Does Alvarez do justice to the achievement of both poets?

2   In *The Ironic Harvest* (1974), Geoffrey Thurley relates Hughes's animal poems to the 'native English tradition' of Lawrence and Hopkins, and also lesser poets such as Edmund Blunden and James Stephens. You might like to discuss the animal poem genre with this approach in mind, starting perhaps with Thurley's comparison between Blunden's 'The Pike' and Hughes's 'Pike' poem. Does Hughes represent an advance on such earlier poetry? Is he close to Lawrence (you might look at 'Humming-bird' in Unit 1, *English Poetry in 1912*, p 22)? Where does he stand in the 'native English tradition'?

3   Do you accept A. E. Dyson's implied criticism (in his article in the Course Reader, p 425), that Hughes's poetry lacks a human perspective; that 'compassion, anger, humility, nostalgia, disgust and the other attitudes belonging to the perspectives of time' are absent from his verse?

4   Does Hughes (like Pound and Yeats) run the danger of hating modern Western civilization so much he turns to a kind of reactionary belief in primitive aristocratic codes, the codes of fascism? You might look at George Orwell's article on Yeats reprinted in the Course Reader, pp 349–54, as well as C. J. Rawson, 'Ted Hughes: A Reappraisal', listed below.

5   ' "Crow's" naturalistic presence, so far as he has one, allows some scope for Hughes's old bestiarizing gifts; his theological presence – he is simultaneously God's partner, God's victim, God's godless Man – is vague and immense enough to permit unlimited portentousness; his human stance – tough, sardonic, blood-soaked – is so deliberately (and fashionably) cartoon-like for it to seem an irrelevance to complain of its utter superficiality.' (Ian Hamilton, 'A Mouthful of Blood', from an anonymous review in the *Times Literary Supplement*.) Is this adequate as a response to *Crow*?

FURTHER READING

If you have the time, and find Hughes's poetry interesting, the first thing I would suggest you do is read more of the poems in the Faber paperback, *Selected Poems: 1957–1967*, and in *Crow* (Faber paperback 1970). You might also like to read further in the collections of Hughes's poems already referred to, *The Hawk in the Rain*, *Lupercal* and *Wodwo*, all easily available in Faber paperbacks. Beyond that, the most useful introductory survey I can recommend is Keith Sagar's little booklet in the 'Writers and their Work' series, *Ted Hughes* (1972) which contains a short bibliography.

Sagar has also written the first book-length study of Hughes's work, entitled *The Art of Ted Hughes*. It is disappointingly uncritical, and, oddly, reads at times as if it were dictated by Hughes himself. But it contains an invaluable account of Hughes's creative career as well as the fullest bibliography yet to appear, an exhaustive list of works by and about Hughes. Sagar tells us about the new sequences of poems since *Crow*, including *Gaudete* (1977), which he hugely overpraises, and *Cave Birds* (1978), another bird-cycle, more abstract than *Crow*, but with drawings by Leonard Baskin.

Important further reading for any study of Hughes's work may be found in his own critical writings: I have already quoted from *Poetry in the Making* and the introduction to *Vasco Popa: Selected Poems*, as well as his introduction to *A Choice of Shakespeare's Verse*, which includes a fascinating 'Note' on the 'fable' underlying Shakespeare's verse. Also worth consulting:
'The Poetry of Keith Douglas', *The Listener*, 21 June 1962.
A Choice of Emily Dickinson's Verse, selected with an introduction by Ted Hughes (Faber paperback 1968).
There are several interviews and autobiographical pieces referred to in Sagar's bibliography, the most important being that with Egbert Faas, 'Ted Hughes and Crow', in the *London Magazine*.

Hughes on record includes:
Listening and Writing, BBC Records, RESR 19M: two talks by Hughes, including readings of 'The Thought-Fox', 'Pike' ,'View of a Pig' and D. H. Lawrence's 'Bare Almond Trees'.
The Poet Speaks, No. 5 Argo PLP 1085, on which the poet reads nine poems from *Wodwo*, and Sylvia Plath reads three from *Ariel*.
Crow, Claddagh CCT 9–10: Hughes reads all but three of the poems in the first English edition of *Crow*.

SELECT CRITICISM AND REFERENCES

Alvarez, A. (1962) *The New Poetry*, Penguin.
Bedient, Calvin 'On Ted Hughes', *Critical Quarterly* XIV (Summer 1972) reprinted in C. Bedient (1974) *Eight Contemporary Poets*, Oxford University Press.
Faas, Egbert 'Ted Hughes and Crow', *London Magazine*, new series X (January 1971), pp 5–20.

Hamburger, Michael (1972) *The Truth of Poetry*, Pelican.

Hamilton, Ian 'A Mouthful of Blood', *Times Literary Supplement*, 8 January 1971 reprinted in I. Hamilton (1973) *A Poetry Chronicle*, Faber.

Hughes, Ted (1967) *Poetry in the Making*, Faber.

Hughes, Ted (1969) Introduction *Vasco Popa: Selected Poems*, Penguin.

Hughes, Ted (1971) *A Choice of Shakespeare's Verse*, Faber.

Lodge, David 'Crow and the Cartoons', *Critical Quarterly* XIII (Spring 1971) reprinted in Jeremy Robson (ed) (1973) *Poetry Dimension I*, Sphere.

Martin, Graham and Furbank, P. N. (eds) (1975) *Twentieth Century Poetry: Critical Essays and Documents*, The Open University Press. (Course Reader)

May, Derwent 'Ted Hughes' in Martin Dodsworth (ed) (1970) *The Survival of Poetry*, Faber. An excellent critical introduction to the poetry before *Crow*.

Press, John (1963) *Rule and Energy*, Oxford University Press. Contains a chapter 'Metaphysics and Mythologies', discussing Hughes's poetry.

Press, John (1969) *A Map of Modern Verse*, Oxford University Press. (Set book)

Rawson, C. J. 'Ted Hughes: A Reappraisal', *Essays in Criticism* XV (January 1965) pp 77–94; attacks Hughes's violence.

Rosenthal, M. L. (1967) *The New Poets*, Oxford University Press. Contains an appreciative essay on Hughes's poetry.

Sagar, Keith (1978) *The Art of Ted Hughes*, Second Edition, Cambridge University Press.

Thurley, Geoffrey (1974) *The Ironic Harvest*, Arnold. Contains a section on Hughes's poetry as creating a revolution in sensibility.

PART 2   SYLVIA PLATH

1   THE MYTH

Figure 3   Sylvia Plath (Courtesy Olwyn Hughes. Photo: Rollie McKenna)

1.1   To get anywhere near the special quality and achievement of Sylvia Plath's poetry
one has to try to demythologize her. Since her suicide early in 1963, her name has
taken on the quality of a legend: inevitably, the sudden end to her life aroused much
morbid curiosity, and still does, although A. Alvarez, her first champion as poetry
editor of the *Observer*, tried to provide a cool if personal account of the last days of
fierce creativity which preceded her death, in his book on suicide, *The Savage God*.
Alvarez tells of a lonely but determined woman who takes her own life almost
accidentally, as the last of a series of gambles with death, but one which she was
doomed to lose. This still seems to leave a lot unanswered, but perhaps that will
always be the case: no account can contain the whole truth. The trouble is, there
remains a residue of uncertainty, even mystery, about her life and work which only
preserves the legendary qualities which have come to surround her, and which
confuses one's response to the poetry. The kind of thing I have in mind has been very

clearly expressed by a reviewer in a recent issue of the *Cambridge Quarterly*. As she puts it, she came under the Plath spell when a young woman, exhibiting what was I'm sure a common response, and not only from sixteen year olds:

> I first read Sylvia Plath four or five years ago, when only *The Colossus*, *Ariel* and *The Bell Jar* were in print, and immediately I took her as my own, because I identified with her. What I didn't identify with, I aspired to. The fact of her having written at all meant a lot then; it meant that a clever woman didn't have to choose exclusively between a gruff, misandrous academicism, and domestic vegetation. Partly it meant that a poem could be burrowing away somewhere while you measured the flour, and so on, but mostly, when you were told that women didn't have the flights of energy and concentration to write poetry, that they wrote compassionate novels that could be popped into the kitchen drawer at a moment's notice, it showed that the energy would last to go further than the minutiae of domesticity and adultery. But none of these estimable qualities would have taken on such validity and urgency if they had not been refracted through a sixteen-year-old's ideas of mental illness, suffering and suicide. It was her suicide that breathed life into the poems, proof that things really *were* that bad . . . (Nash '*A Closer Look at Ariel* by Nancy Hunter Steiner' *Cambridge Quarterly*.)

The confusion of the myth and the poetry seems pretty clear, I think.

1.2   Alvarez in fact initiated some of this confusion by certain grim remarks uttered in a memorial broadcast on the BBC Third Programme very shortly after the poet's death. This broadcast, which eventually became the well-known article published in *The Review* (and reprinted in your Course Reader, pp 432–9), was partly a tribute and partly a guide to reading her last strange poems; but it concluded with the portentous words: 'Poetry of this order is a murderous art.' Later, in a postscript published in *Tri Quarterly* in 1966, Alvarez admitted that he might have added to the confusion between the myth and the reality of Sylvia Plath, even helping to encourage the idea which had since gained much ground, that her final breakdown and death in some way validated the extreme, emotional quality of her writing. He went on to elaborate a theory of what he called 'Extremist' poetry, a poetry which was deeply committed to an exploration of the hidden roots of fear, guilt and anxiety which lie within the individual psyche and which also reflect the darkly hostile forces at work in society at large. 'The Extremist artist sets out deliberately to explore the roots of his emotions, the obscurest springs of his personality, maybe even the sickness he feels himself prey to . . .' (Alvarez *Beyond All This Fiddle*, pp 57–8.)

1.3   It should already be clear how a poet such as Ted Hughes might be said to fit this theory. And it is no coincidence that Hughes turned out to be one of those whom Alvarez saw as a leading exponent of 'Extremist' poetry, and whom he had praised in his introduction to the Penguin anthology, *The New Poetry*. The others were all Americans: Robert Lowell, John Berryman and Sylvia Plath. In these terms, Hughes becomes of vital importance as a transmitter to the English poetic scene of a peculiarly American ability to reinvoke the 'modernist' tradition of experimentation as a means of coping with the distress and unease of modern life. This may be seen as very much Alvarez's idea, an idea rooted in his own personal preference for a poetry which, as he put it, went beyond the 'gentility principle' by renewing the 'modernist' impulse towards creating verse which dealt with disturbance and breakdown by means of immensely skilful technical devices, such as Eliot's mask of impersonality. The 'gentility principle', according to Alvarez, was what informed English poetry of the fifties, poetry dominated by a tame empiricism, distrustful of emotion and rhetoric, and exemplified by the Movement. The awful reality of twentieth century life was passed by. Again, the crucial contrast was between Philip Larkin's 'At Grass' and Hughes's 'A Dream of Horses'. Hughes's poetry was welcomed as signalling the reappearance of serious, powerful and disturbing poetry, poetry which plumbed the depths of the modern psyche. Interestingly, Alvarez did not include Sylvia Plath's work in the first edition of his *The New Poetry*, although she was brought in later; yet it was, according to Alvarez, this essay of his (and perhaps also a sympathetic review of *The Colossus*), which made her come to him with her *Ariel* poems: 'Apparently, this essay said something she wished to hear; she spoke of it after and with approval, and was disappointed not to have been included among the poets in the book'. (Alvarez *The Savage God*, p 40.)

1.4 In Alvarez's view (and Alvarez has been widely influential), it is specifically Sylvia Plath's later poems which reveal the 'Extremist' impulse in its purest or most 'final' form. There is only one way of testing the truth of this, and that is to look at the poems themselves. This is also the only way to discover whether or not the 'Extremist' impulse leads to good or effective writing in poetry. But to look only at the late poems, the poems of *Ariel* or *Winter Trees* (1971), is in fact to accept one aspect of the Plath myth unexamined: the assumption that only in that kind of poetry did she reveal her most important or 'best' abilities. So one ought to begin by looking at some of her earlier work as well. It may be that there is a unity, a continuity in her work which it is too easy to miss if one simply looks at the most famous, late pieces. In an article of crucial importance to any reader of her work who wishes to study it in any depth, Ted Hughes concluded that, surveyed as a whole, 'the unity of her opus is clear.' (Hughes 'Notes on the Chronological Order of Sylvia Plath's Poems' in *The Art of Sylvia Plath* ed Newman, p 195.)

2 'METAPHORS'

2.1 I would like to begin with a poem not very familiar to the Plath mythologists, but one which does perhaps reveal something of the nature of her craft and concerns. It is taken from *The Colossus*, her first collection (although she had been writing poetry for many years), which appeared shortly after her return from America with Ted Hughes early in 1960. It was the only collection of Sylvia Plath's poetry to be published during her life time. It contained some fifty poems, including the following, 'Metaphors', which you might like to read now.

■ How does it compare with the work we have been looking at by Ted Hughes, in tone and in subject?

Metaphors

I'm a riddle in nine syllables,
An elephant, a ponderous house,
A melon strolling on two tendrils. ←
O red fruit, ivory, fine timbers!
This loaf's big with its yeasty rising.
Money's new-minted in this fat purse.
I'm a means, a stage, a cow in calf.
I've eaten a bag of green apples,
Boarded the train there's no getting off.

Discussion

2.2 Perhaps the first thing you might have noticed is that this poem doesn't have quite the immediate impact or accessibility of Ted Hughes's poetry. Simply, it's more difficult. The surface is puzzling, opaque, a bit enigmatic in what you might feel is a rather self-conscious way. At the same time, it is surely a dazzling exercise in manipulating language, enjoying, and apparently asking us to enjoy, a sheer creative inventiveness expressed in a rush of metaphor. But what is it all about? The seventh line seems to give the game away: 'I'm a means, a stage, a cow in calf.' That is, she is pregnant. And perhaps pregnant with language as well as with child. All the 'metaphors' illustrate pregnancy, are fertile in some sense. This is obviously a more revealing and personal topic than we have met with in Ted Hughes; yet it is treated with a lightness of touch, a deft, humorous detachment which hardly coincides with the image of a woman delving into the extremes of personal feeling which one might have been led to expect from Alvarez's remarks. Comedy is not absent from Ted Hughes's work, although if you look at the 'Crow' cycle, it becomes clear that his humour is of a black, ferocious and cosmic cast. But Sylvia Plath is capable of a remarkably light, self-mocking humour, not only in *The Colossus* but in poems collected after her death in *Crossing the Water* (1971) and even in *Ariel* and *Winter Trees*. ∎

2.3 Such humour tends to revolve around explorations of her own bodily processes, although there is also an amusing, Hughesian poem in *The Colossus* called 'Sow', comprising a witty meditation upon that gross beast, no 'rose-and-larkspurred china suckling/With a penny slot', more like a 'vast/Brobdingnag bulk', a 'vision of ancient hoghood'. More typical are those poems which reflect an amused, slightly fearful fascination with her body, a kind of poetry of the *viscera*, such as 'Cut' in *Ariel*, which opens: 'What a thrill –/My thumb instead of an onion', and goes on to take up the everyday, domestic incident with an astonishingly inventive series of exaggerated mock-heroic metaphors:

Cut

For Susan O'Neill Roe

What a thrill——
My thumb instead of an onion.
The top quite gone
Except for a sort of a hinge

Of skin,
A flap like a hat,
Dead white.
Then that red plush.

Little pilgrim,
The Indian's axed your scalp.
Your turkey wattle
Carpet rolls

Straight from the heart.
I step on it,
Clutching my bottle
Of pink fizz.

A celebration, this is.
Out of a gap
A million soldiers run,
Redcoats, every one.

34

Whose side are they on?
O my
Homunculus, I am ill.
I have taken a pill to kill

The thin
Papery feeling.
Saboteur,
Kamikaze man——

The stain on your
Gauze Ku Klux Klan
Babushka
Darkens and tarnishes and when

The balled
Pulp of your heart
Confronts its small
Mill of silence

How you jump——
Trepanned veteran,
Dirty girl,
Thumb stump.

2.4 It is all a little narcissistic, but the poet's detachment makes this acceptable, and a legitimate means of establishing the first, acutely physical impression which can then be deepened into greater significance, as in the poem ostensibly about a bruise, 'Contusion' (also in *Ariel*). Associated with such poetry are several poems about being in hospital, about the condition of being 'In Plaster', for instance (the condition of a woman in a bed near her own, as it happens, when she was recovering from an appendectomy): 'I shall never get out of this! There are two of me now:/This new absolutely white person and the old yellow one' (*Crossing the Water*). The humour becomes grimmer, more macabre, however, as the sense or threat of death overtakes her; yet it is a threat present in her poetry from the start, as in 'Two Views of a Cadaver Room' (in *The Colossus*), where we are asked to contemplate the bodies laid out 'black as burnt turkey', and the 'snail-nosed babies' which 'moon and glow' in their jars nearby:

Two Views of a Cadaver Room

1
The day she visited the dissecting room
They had four men laid out, black as burnt turkey,
Already half unstrung. A vinegary fume
Of the death vats clung to them;
The white-smocked boys started working.
The head of his cadaver had caved in,
And she could scarcely make out anything
In that rubble of skull plates and old leather.
A sallow piece of string held it together.

In their jars the snail-nosed babies moon and glow.
He hands her the cut-out heart like a cracked heirloom.

Figure 4 Breughel the Elder The Triumph of Death – *detail from bottom right of painting* (Prado. Photo: Mansell Collection)

2

In Brueghel's panorama of smoke and slaughter
Two people only are blind to the carrion army:
He, afloat in the sea of her blue satin
Skirts, sings in the direction
Of her bare shoulder, while she bends,
Fingering a leaflet of music, over him,
Both of them deaf to the fiddle in the hands
Of the death's-head shadowing their song.
These Flemish lovers flourish; not for long.

Yet desolation, stalled in paint, spares the little country
Foolish, delicate, in the lower right hand corner.

2.5 But 'Metaphors' avoids these more frightening areas, preferring the playful and humorous touch. You will notice that it pretends to be a riddle ('I'm a riddle in nine syllables'). This tells us something of the poet's characteristic strategy towards her readers, as well as being an apt allusion to children's games. And this strategy is, not to yield up her meaning too easily or quickly, but to make you, the reader, work to reach the sometimes very private world of her poems. If the poem's world remains private, one can – and should, perhaps – question this 'obscurity'. There are certainly times when this happens; as it happens in Pound say, or Robert Lowell too. But in 'Metaphors', my feeling is that the initial 'obscurity' is part of the pleasure. We share, as we are meant to, the poet's own surprise at the comic, cumbersome and puzzling object she has become, an object which also as it were surprises the metaphors which she brings in to try and capture its essence. It is both absurd and touching, the conception (in every sense) of herself as, for instance, a 'melon strolling on two tendrils', like in some child's drawing of its mother.

In a sense, 'Metaphors' gives us a child's eye view. The riddle is played out as in a nursery game, with a list of attributes, some apparently most arbitrary in their association with the subject. It is a method used with similar aptness in a later and more finely achieved poem, 'You're', written just before the birth of her daughter Frieda in 1960, and the earliest of the poems to be collected later in *Ariel*. 'You're' rings the changes on lively, affectionate and humorous metaphors:

You're

Clownlike, happiest on your hands,
Feet to the stars, and moon-skulled,
Gilled like a fish. A common-sense
Thumbs-down on the dodo's mode.
Wrapped up in yourself like a spool,
Trawling your dark as owls do.
Mute as a turnip from the Fourth
Of July to All Fools' Day,
O high-riser, my little loaf.

Vague as fog and looked for like mail.
Farther off than Australia.
Bent-backed Atlas, our travelled prawn.
Snug as a bud and at home
Like a sprat in a pickle jug.
A creel of eels, all ripples.
Jumpy as a Mexican bean.
Right, like a well-done sum.
A clean slate, with your own face on.

2.6 'You're' is in syllabics, a form unusual for *Ariel*, but much more common in her earlier verse. Thus 'Metaphors', as it informs us, consists of nine nine-syllable lines. Elsewhere in *The Colossus* there is an even more intricately shaped poem, 'Aftermath', a sonnet in syllabics, nine to the line. It is as if Sylvia Plath were proving how successfully she could handle the difficult modern form so brilliantly exploited by Dylan Thomas in 'Poem in October' or 'Fern Hill'. Whereas, as we have seen, Ted Hughes chose to break away from traditional metrical patterns by moving towards a stress-based line, it is notable that Sylvia Plath chose to do so by trying something more difficult, crafty, and consciously contrived. Not for her (at first) the inevitably high emotional charge of powerful, close-packed rhythms; rather the quieter, more intellectual and detached mood generated by these carefully-spaced syllabics. Underlying 'Metaphors', one can feel an iambic-anapaestic swing, but it is subtle, barely perceptible. More noticeable is the clever hint of patterning in the rhyme-scheme, although that is also almost hidden, oblique ('syllables' and 'tendrils', 'calf' and 'off', and 'rising' rhyming internally with 'getting'). Less interested than Thomas or Ted Hughes in words which mime action by means of sound and rhythm, she seems to prefer a sharp, witty accumulation of meaning by creating striking new metaphors which yoke together otherwise apparently distant ideas and associations. This is a manner reminiscent of an earlier period, of the Elizabethans and Jacobeans, as the allusion in line eight of 'Metaphors' to the common belief of their time that eating green fruit revealed pregnancy might suggest. 'Metaphors' like 'You're', is a 'conceit'.

3 THE COLOSSUS

3.1 The dominant tone of 'Metaphors' may be playful and affectionate, but this is not true of the collection in which it is found, although there is more wit and humour in it (and in most of her poetry) than is generally recognized. In fact, to look at the last line of 'Metaphors', you might suspect a slightly chilling overtone, an implication that the pregnant body is somehow like an uncontrollable machine, taking her willy-nilly along its own way and according to its own purposes – perhaps a very accurate reflection of what it felt like to be pregnant for the first time, as she was.

A more serious and perhaps characteristic poem, which steers more closely towards the painfully personal area of her life, but with a similar high sense of craft and control, might be the title poem of her first collection. It is in some ways even more startlingly inventive, yet disciplined, than any we have touched on so far; and it helps to introduce a dominant theme of her work. Here it is:

The Colossus

I shall never get you put together entirely,
Pieced, glued, and properly jointed.
Mule-bray, pig-grunt and bawdy cackles
Proceed from your great lips.
It's worse than a barnyard.

Perhaps you consider yourself an oracle,
Mouthpiece of the dead, or of some god or other.
Thirty years now I have laboured
To dredge the silt from your throat.
I am none the wiser.

Scaling little ladders with gluepots and pails of lysol
I crawl like an ant in mourning
Over the weedy acres of your brow
To mend the immense skull-plates and clear
The bald, white tumuli of your eyes.

A blue sky out of the Oresteia
Arches above us. O father, all by yourself
You are pithy and historical as the Roman Forum.
I open my lunch on a hill of black cypress.
Your fluted bones and acanthine hair are littered

In their old anarchy to the horizon-line.
It would take more than a lightning-stroke
To create such a ruin.
Nights, I squat in the cornucopia
Of your left ear, out of the wind,

Counting the red stars and those of plum-colour.
The sun rises under the pillar of your tongue.
My hours are married to shadow.
No longer do I listen for the scrape of a keel
On the blank stones of the landing.

This may seem initially even more of a riddle than 'Metaphors'. Perhaps it would be a help to remind you that the colossus which provides the basic metaphoric scheme of the poem is derived from that giant statue of the sun-god, which passed for one of the seven wonders of the world and which, according to popular tradition, bestrode the entrance of the harbour at Rhodes, its feet resting on the two moles, enabling ships to pass between its legs. The actual statue (which was only 102 feet high and probably not even erected at the harbour) was demolished by an earthquake. It may be that this is the most important thing about the statue in this poem: it is in ruins, after a catastrophic collapse, a scattered pile of remains over which the narrator clambers hopelessly trying to put it together again. (You might like to look up for yourself any words which still puzzle you, including the allusion to the *Oresteia*.)

■ But what is the poem *really* about, do you think? Keep in mind Sylvia Plath's penchant for exploring a personal, intimate theme obliquely, by means of metaphors, and look most closely at the fourth stanza, which perhaps provides the most obvious clue to the poem's meaning. What do the last three lines imply?

Discussion

3.2 That cry in the fourth stanza, 'O father', helps us to realize that the helpless, absorbed figure depicted crawling ant-like and industrious over the mammoth ruin of her god, is a child searching for her dead father among the fragments of the past. To read Sylvia Plath's poems is to come to this kind of realization over and over again: the Father is always, on some level, her father. Sometimes the metaphor is more explicit: there is a poem in *The Colossus* called 'The Beekeeper's Daughter' which Ted Hughes described as one of a group of poems written about her father, who used to keep bees. In 'The Beekeeper's Daughter', she refers to herself thus: 'My heart under your foot, sister of a stone', suggesting her sense of infinite smallness beside her father, and submission to her image of him. Later, in her most well-known poem, 'Daddy' (see para 4.3) she alludes to him as 'Ghastly statue with one grey toe/Big as a Frisco seal'. She is so often the child, tiny, vulnerable (or, as in 'Daddy', angry), searching for this massive, solid figure in some insubstantial world of her own. Her father dead, the search must always be fruitless, as 'The Colossus' implies. ■

3.3 In fact, Sylvia Plath's father died after a lengthy illness when she was nine, an event which undoubtedly had immense, disturbing significance in her life, and which dominated her work. 'My German-speaking father', she tells us as Esther Greenwood in *The Bell Jar*, 'came from some manic-depressive hamlet in the black heart of Prussia.' This was Grabow, in the Polish corridor, from which Otto Plath emigrated to America as a youth, to become professor of biology at Boston University, marrying Aurelia Schober, a first-generation American of Austrian descent, and forming a household in which intellectual rigour and competitiveness was a keynote. When, in *The Bell Jar*, Esther Greenwood decides to visit the grave of her father for the first time, as her own mental condition is worsening, she remarks that the graveyard and even his death had seemed unreal to her since she was a child, when, she says, her mother had not let her come to the funeral. And so 'I had a great yearning, lately, to pay my father back for all the years of regret, and start tending his grave. I had always been my father's favourite, and it seemed fitting I should take on a mourning my mother had never bothered with.'

3.4 Thus, now, in 'The Colossus', 'I crawl like an ant in mourning/Over the weedy acres of your brow'. And if, at first, the broken statue seems comic, absurd, with those 'bawdy cackles' proceeding from its great lips and sounding 'worse than a barnyard', we realize there is something deeply serious and disturbing underlying this. In 'Poem for a Birthday', the poet warns, 'Mother, keep out of my barnyard'. It is as if the careless, busy, domestic creatures at the beginning of 'The Colossus' represent a mockery of the impotent dead, an idea which obscurely relates to her mother's real or imagined unconcern over her father's death. The possibility of there being such an undercurrent of resentful, even aggressive emotions in the title poem is reinforced by her allusion to the *Oresteia* in stanza four, indirectly suggesting bloody, familial conflict and murder.[1] But this explicitness she dared not use until 'Daddy', and even in that poem, as we shall see, the personal anguish is apparently distanced by various devices, including historical references, which seem to take over the function of the classical, mythological allusions in 'The Colossus'.

What makes 'The Colossus' a fine poem, in my view, is that it maintains the inexplicitness which Sylvia Plath was later to discard. The emotions are generalized by her indirectness, which makes it possible for us to share the deep and painful feelings hovering about the poem. Thus we can share the child's desire for security so effectively caught in that image of herself at night, able to do no more than 'squat in the cornucopia/Of your left ear, out of the wind', counting the stars, barely sheltered by the fragments of what once filled her world 'to the horizon-line'. Yet it is this desire for security and protection which drives her into the hopeless task of resurrecting her dead father. The hopelessness of the task finally becomes a dreadful, inescapable servitude, which it may indeed have been for Sylvia Plath, if her obsession with the subject is anything to go by; and this is revealed in the note of empty despair on which the poem ends:

> My hours are married to shadow.
> No longer do I listen for the scrape of a keel
> On the blank stones of the landing.

When the colossus stood, all-powerful and massive, she was able to move away from it, protected by the immense being. Now that it has collapsed, it is only a shadow, a memory which haunts and traps her in the harbour which imprisons rather than protects.

As far as the form of the poem is concerned, it is notable that the rather self-conscious virtuosity of 'Metaphors' and many of the other poems in the collection, is here modified by a more relaxed and colloquial tone, the sentences running on beyond one or two lines, the length of line varying considerably, and with barely a hint of rhyme. It is left to the inner logic of accumulated images to hold the poem together. Yet it is still not a poem to be read aloud for the whip and sting of sound enacting meaning, although there are some cleverly reinforcing usages ('bawdy cackles', for instance, or 'the scrape of a keel'). The poet admitted later she could not read any of the poems from *The Colossus* out loud herself; but, 'I didn't write them to be read aloud.' (Orr *The Poet Speaks* p 170: an interview.) In general, there is an air of studied meditation about them, corresponding to what Nancy Hunter Steiner said of her friend's early methods of composition, 'plodding through dictionary and thesaurus for the exact word to create the poetic effect she intended'. (Hunter Steiner *A Closer Look at Ariel*, p 21.) Hardly the spontaneous overflow of strong feeling; but Sylvia Plath had reason to resist this, even if it meant introducing

---

[1]In an uncollected poem of this time, it is all made much more explicit: the poem is entitled 'Electra on Azalea Path', and it reveals her guilt, the child's guilt that it has in some way killed the dead parent, and which helps to explain the obsession with destruction and hostility projected onto the parent or onto oneself—or both:

> Oh pardon the one who knocks for pardon at
> Your gate, father—your hound-bitch, daughter, friend.
> It was my love that did us both to death.

'Electra on Azalea Path', *Hudson Review*, Vol. XIII (Fall 1960), p 415.

In the *Oresteia* by Aeschylus, Electra is the daughter of King Agamemnon, who is murdered by his wife, Clytemnestra, herself later killed by her son, Orestes.

sometimes oddly esoteric or archaic terms, words such as 'ruddled' or 'maundering', as in the aureate, Wallace Stevens-like fancy, 'Ouija'. ('Fluted', or 'acanthine' in 'The Colossus' are apt and precise architectural terms.)

3.5 In the end, as with any poet, it's not so much the choice of rare diction which matters, as the way in which it is used. 'Maundering' (which means to ramble along in a dreamy, inconsequent way), is exactly the kind of word which adds richness to the texture of, for instance, Robert Lowell's verse. In fact, he has a line, 'Crows maunder on the petrified fairway', in 'Waking in the Blue', from *Life Studies* – a group of poems which encouraged Sylvia Plath to write the kind of dense and brilliantly rich verse we find in *The Colossus*, if not to draw on the same word in a poem. In 'Point Shirley', an elegy to her dead grandmother and the savage sea which used to pound her grandmother's house on the New England shore, she writes of the 'gritted wave' which 'leaps/The seawall and drops onto a bier/Of quahog chips,/Leaving a salty mash of ice . . . ', of the 'collusion of mulish elements' against her grandmother, of 'A thresh-tailed, lanced/Shark littered in the geranium bed'; all very close to the subject, mood and manner of Lowell's elegies on his family, of the sounding splash and shock of verbal inventiveness which dominates, for instance, his 'Quaker Graveyard in Nantucket'. And, as it happens, while Sylvia Plath and her husband were living in Boston (1958 – summer 1959), during the period of the composition of many of the poems in *The Colossus*, she began to attend Lowell's poetry classes at the university there, according to Ted Hughes writing 'Point Shirley' as a 'deliberate exercise' in Lowell's 'early style'. (Hughes in Newman *The Art of Sylvia Plath*, p 191.) Afterwards, she was to say how 'very excited' she had been made by the 'new breakthrough' which came with *Life Studies*, 'this intense breakthrough into very serious, very personal, emotional experience which I feel has been partly taboo.' (Course Reader, p 435.)

3.6 What she meant by 'taboo' experience was Lowell's treatment of his personal history of mental illness in *Life Studies*. Yet it seems an exaggeration to suggest that this kind of subject *was* taboo: on one level at least, *The Waste Land* was an expression of mental breakdown on Eliot's part, if covertly and indirectly so; and Nerval, Rimbaud and the French Surrealists had anticipated this development (if not influenced it) by exploring extreme psychological states in their verse and prose poems. To take an even longer perspective, one could say that it was in any case a characteristic of Romantic poetry to be interested in the further recesses of the mind, although it is necessary to draw a distinction between the nature of their concerns and that of the 'moderns': in a poem such as John Clare's 'I am', written during the last, only intermittently sane years of his life (he died in 1864), the poet's experience of madness and loss of identity is expressed along with a conviction that there is an unfragmented reality existing outside his own private, disturbed world.[2] The 'modern' assumption has been that reality itself is questionable, a condition of the individual consciousness which is essentially in a state of neurosis, disorder or alienation. Perhaps the most important point to be made here is simply that what Lowell did was lift a taboo which Sylvia Plath felt existed *for her*: he gave her the example which enabled her to break out of her own restricted outlook on what she felt was permissible or 'poetic'.

With the appearance of Lowell's *Life Studies* in 1959, there arose what was labelled by the American critic, M. L. Rosenthal, a poetry of 'confession', the poetry of John Berryman, Anne Sexton and Sylvia Plath, and others liberated by Lowell.[3] As Barry Chambers has suggested in Unit 27 *Robert Lowell*, the epithet 'confessional' can be misleading, and we need to remember that it can be used to refer loosely to

[2] 'I am' may be found in the *Penguin Book of English Romantic Verse*, ed. David Wright (1968), pp 272–3, and similar anthologies.
[3] See Rosenthal's section on 'Robert Lowell and the Poetry of Confession' in his book (on your Further Reading List for this course), *The Modern Poets: A Critical Introduction* (Oxford, 1960, many later editions, including a paperback reprint, 1972), pp 225–44.

the personal content of a poem when it is also a matter of form, or method. But for Sylvia Plath, this new, more nakedly personal poetry dealing with experiences of mental disorder helped free her for the creation of a newly uncompromising style of verse which dealt more directly with the subject matter which she felt was closest to her, and which she was to explore increasingly in her extraordinary last poems. The emergence of this new kind of poetry occurs in the final sequence of poems in *The Colossus* called 'Poem for a Birthday'. It is significant that this is a *sequence* rather than a single poem, exploring different points of view just as Lowell or Eliot and Pound had done.

3.7 'Poem for a Birthday' is an extraordinary and powerful poem, if somewhat obscure, expressing various states of mind associated with Sylvia Plath's pregnancy, parents, madness and final tentative recovery. Each of these states emerges as part of a separate monologue. I would like to look in particular at the last section, entitled 'The Stones': in this, we have the culmination of what is happening in *The Colossus*, and at the same time a decisive turn towards the world of *Ariel* and her last poems.

The Stones

This is the city where men are mended.
I lie on a great anvil.
The flat blue sky-circle

Flew off like the hat of a doll
When I fell out of the light. I entered
The stomach of indifference, the wordless cupboard.

The mother of pestles diminished me.
I became a still pebble.
The stones of the belly were peaceable,

The head-stone quiet, jostled by nothing.
Only the mouth-hole piped out,
Importunate cricket

In a quarry of silences.
The people of the city heard it.
They hunted the stones, taciturn and separate,

The mouth-hole crying their locations.
Drunk as a foetus
I suck at the paps of darkness.

The food tubes embrace me. Sponges kiss my lichens away.
The jewelmaster drives his chisel to pry
Open one stone eye.

This is the after-hell: I see the light.
A wind unstoppers the chamber
Of the ear, old worrier.

Water mollifies the flint lip,
And daylight lays its sameness on the wall.
The grafters are cheerful,

Heating the pincers, hoisting the delicate hammers.
A current agitates the wires
Volt upon volt. Catgut stitches my fissures.

A workman walks by carrying a pink torso.
The storerooms are full of hearts.
This is the city of spare parts.

My swaddled legs and arms smell sweet as rubber.
Here they can doctor heads, or any limb.
On Fridays the little children come

To trade their hooks for hands.
Dead men leave eyes for others.
Love is the uniform of my bald nurse.

Love is the bone and sinew of my curse.
The vase, reconstructed, houses
The elusive rose.

Ten fingers shape a bowl for shadows.
My mendings itch. There is nothing to do.
I shall be good as new.

Thus, 'The Stones' begins by revealing that now it is *she* who needs mending, not that projected image of her long-dead father made visible as a cracked colossus; we are taken behind the walls of the mental hospital, to where she lies after her first suicide attempt:

This is the city were men are mended.
I lie on a great anvil.
The flat blue sky-circle

Flew off like the hat of a doll
When I fell out of the light. I entered
The stomach of indifference, the wordless cupboard.

This is abrupt, painful, nightmarish. The blue sky links back to 'The Colossus', but now there is no large, metaphoric indirection, indeed we have entered a private world in which much that is enigmatic may remain so. One way of penetrating the enigma is to become aware of the persistence of echoes from other poems, the obsessional return to clusters of typical imagery. The doll is a common image, and it is entirely characteristic that something with comfortable, homely and childish associations should become unpleasant, sinister. Elsewhere, in 'The Disquieting Muses', she sees her childish powers of imagination represented in three dolls nodding their heads around her crib, three ladies 'Mouthless, eyeless, with stitched bald head'. This image is not as private as it may seem at first, either: the muses are of course classical deities of creativity, but more important, I think, is the fact (which I am convinced must be more than chance) that her title echoes precisely that of a painting by de Chirico, the Italian surrealist. For the surreal element is strong in her work, her metaphorical playfulness is part of a visionary, primitive tendency to juxtapose apparently unconnected things in a fantastic world which only makes sense in states of dream or reverie. Here is 'The Disquieting Muses':

The Disquieting Muses

Mother, mother, what illbred aunt
Or what disfigured and unsightly
Cousin did you so unwisely keep
Unasked to my christening, that she
Sent these ladies in her stead
With heads like darning-eggs to nod
And nod and nod at foot and head
And at the left side of my crib?

43

Mother, who made to order stories
Of Mixie Blackshort the heroic bear,
Mother, whose witches always, always
Got baked into gingerbread, I wonder
Whether you saw them, whether you said
Words to rid me of those three ladies
Nodding by night around my bed,
Mouthless, eyeless, with stitched bald head.

In the hurricane, when father's twelve
Study windows bellied in
Like bubbles about to break, you fed
My brother and me cookies and ovaltine
And helped the two of us to choir:
'Thor is angry: boom boom boom!
Thor is angry: we don't care!'
But those ladies broke the panes.

When on tiptoe the schoolgirls danced,
Blinking flashlights like fireflies
And singing the glowworm song, I could
Not lift a foot in the twinkle-dress
But, heavy-footed, stood aside
In the shadow cast by my dismal-headed
Godmothers, and you cried and cried:
And the shadow stretched, the lights went out.

Mother, you sent me to piano lessons
And praised my arabesques and trills
Although each teacher found my touch
Oddly wooden in spite of scales
And the hours of practising, my ear
Tone-deaf and yes, unteachable.
I learned, I learned, I learned elsewhere,
From muses unhired by you, dear mother.

I woke one day to see you, mother,
Floating above me in bluest air
On a green balloon bright with a million
Flowers and bluebirds that never were
Never, never, found anywhere.
But the little planet bobbed away
Like a soap-bubble as you called: Come here!
And I faced my travelling companions.

Day now, night now, at head, side, feet,
They stand their vigil in gowns of stone,
Faces blank as the day I was born,
Their shadows long in the setting sun
That never brightens or goes down.
And this is the kingdom you bore me to,
Mother, mother. But no frown of mine
Will betray the company I keep.

3.8 Like Ted Hughes, who referred to the 'underground, primitive drama' of 'The Stones', which he said she wrote in a new, improvisatory way under the excitement of discovering Paul Radin's collection of African folktales (*The Art of Sylvia Plath*, p 192), Sylvia Plath is intent upon penetrating the everyday world in which we live most of the time by invoking the super-real, or surreal world of the unconscious. But she goes further than Hughes, or at least the Hughes with which we are familiar up to now, because she is more acutely personal and revealing, because her 'myths' are less familiar, more her own. She dares more – but can therefore also lose more, by not making herself understood. Like the surrealists, primitive art excites her (as it does Ted Hughes: see *Crow*), but only in so far as it stimulates her to tap her own nightmares. The shattered figure on a landscape is reminiscent of Dali, the bald heads of de Chirico, the free-floating parts she sees everywhere (the city of 'The Stones' is a 'city of spare parts', hearts, legs, heads) of Yves Tanguy; but the experience

Figure 5 Yves Tanguy Mama, Papa is wounded! *1927. Oil on canvas, 36¼″ × 28¾″.* (Collection, The Museum of Modern Art, New York. *c* 1976 S.P.A.D.E.M. Paris)

of personal disintegration is her own. Her madness brings a nightmare distortion of reality; but to come out of it is to salvage some insight into that reality, which is nearer and more pervasive than we like to accept. In 'The Stones', help is at hand: 'The grafters are cheerful', and 'Catgut stitches my fissures' (no lack of emphatic rhythm and alliteration to reinforce this). And she concludes with hope: 'I shall be as good as new'.

4 ARIEL

4.1 But to become 'as good as new', the poet finds impossible. She must be reborn. But what does that imply? Going further still into horror, into the horror within herself. This is where she tries to go in *Ariel*'s most extreme poems, in 'Lady Lazarus', for example.

Of this poem, Sylvia Plath wrote: 'The speaker is a woman who has the great and terrible gift of being reborn. The only trouble is, she has to die first. She is the phoenix, the libertarian spirit, what you will. She is also just a good, plain, resourceful woman.' (Quoted in Rosenthal *The New Poets*, p 82.)

■ Do these comments do it justice? What do you make of it?

Lady Lazarus

I have done it again.
One year in every ten
I manage it ——

A sort of walking miracle, my skin
Bright as a Nazi lampshade,
My right foot

A paperweight,
My face a featureless, fine
Jew linen.

Peel off the napkin
O my enemy.
Do I terrify? ——

The nose, the eye pits, the full set of teeth?
The sour breath
Will vanish in a day.

Soon, soon the flesh
The grave cave ate will be
At home on me

And I a smiling woman.
I am only thirty.
And like the cat I have nine times to die.

This is Number Three.
What a trash
To annihilate each decade.

What a million filaments.
The peanut-crunching crowd
Shoves in to see

Them unwrap me hand and foot ——
The big strip tease.
Gentlemen, ladies

These are my hands
My knees.
I may be skin and bone,

Nevertheless, I am the same, identical woman.
The first time it happened I was ten.
It was an accident.

The second time I meant
To last it out and not come back at all.
I rocked shut

As a seashell.
They had to call and call
And pick the worms off me like sticky pearls.

Dying
Is an art, like everything else.
I do it exceptionally well.

I do it so it feels like hell.
I do it so it feels real.
I guess you could say I've a call.

It's easy enough to do it in a cell.
It's easy enough to do it and stay put.
It's the theatrical

Comeback in broad day
To the same place, the same face, the same brute
Amused shout:

'A miracle!'
That knocks me out.
There is a charge

For the eyeing of my scars, there is a charge
For the hearing of my heart ——
It really goes.

And there is a charge, a very large charge
For a word or a touch
Or a bit of blood

Or a piece of my hair or my clothes.
So, so, Herr Doktor.
So, Herr Enemy.

I am your opus,
I am your valuable,
The pure gold baby

That melts to a shriek.
I turn and burn.
Do not think I underestimate your great concern.

Ash, ash ——
You poke and stir.
Flesh, bone, there is nothing there ——

A cake of soap,
A wedding ring,
A gold filling.

Herr God, Herr Lucifer
Beware
Beware.

Out of the ash
I rise with my red hair
And I eat men like air.

Discussion

4.2 Of course, it *is* shocking, all the more so for one's awareness that it is almost literally true that she had 'done it again', and arisen from death (hence 'Lady Lazarus') by surviving suicide, and that she had done so more than once: the 'accident' when she was ten was a near-drowning; the 'second time', when she really meant not to 'come back at all', was in 1953, when she became severely depressed, took a large number of sleeping pills, and hid herself in a cellar beneath the house, where she was lucky to be found alive three days later; and, more recently, she had 'done it again', by driving off the road deliberately, and then surviving that too. Moreover, as we are only too aware, in the end she lost this game with death, if that is what it is.

But of what relevance are these autobiographical details? One cannot avoid them in discussing Sylvia Plath, they are too easily available. But ought one then simply to dismiss them? Perhaps one ought to try. For the poet herself refers in her remarks on the poem to its 'speaker', not herself, 'a good, plain, resourceful woman', clearly in an attempt to objectify the experience it contains, and to imply that its claim must be to a more than merely immediately personal, literal truth. In his article in your Course Reader (pp 436–7), Alvarez quotes Sylvia Plath saying that although her poems 'come immediately out of the sensuous and emotional experiences I have . . . I believe that one should be able to control and manipulate experiences, even the most terrifying.' How is this control present in 'Lady Lazarus'? Initially, surely, as it is in the poems we have already looked at, by means of metaphoric transformation, and by her sardonically humorous tone. Death becomes a doctor in a Nazi concentration camp, so that instead of the more distant, mythological feel engendered by an image such as the colossus, we are confronted with an all-too-familiar historical occasion, an occasion of one of the most extreme and appalling conceptions of death in our time. Her sense of personal disintegration in death is generalized by allusions to the notorious Nazi commandant who had a lampshade made out of human skin, by allusions to the pitiful remains in the Nazi incinerators: 'A wedding ring,/A gold filling'. At the same time, the personal impulse to death is shown to be an obscene desire to be sensational, 'the theatrical comeback' with a 'big strip tease', thus introducing a mocking self-criticism which helps further to impersonalize the poem, and remove it from self-indulgence. She is, it seems, *diagnosing* the theatrical impulse in suicide, suggesting that the would-be suicide intends to survive and astound everybody. Only extraordinary daring and toughness allows this kind of poetry to emerge, one tells oneself.

And yet . . . is there not something more to be said? Or should one leave writing so horrific to have its impact and be done? Perhaps you should answer these questions for yourself. All I can say is that I am left uneasy by the very brilliance with which 'Lady Lazarus' succeeds, by the crafty originality which deploys irony and metaphor so effectively with such subject matter, by the staggering control which invests it with so shockingly appropriate a mix of slangy American and innocent nursery rhyme tones, by the final jaunty surrealist touch as 'I rise with my red hair/And I eat men like air'. Who can become stronger than God, than Lucifer – than death itself? Why, only death, of course, and so you 'win' by becoming death – or dead. The jauntiness covers an ultimate despair, but I am uncertain if there is any redeeming awareness of this despair here. ■

4.3   Another poem in *Ariel*, is 'Daddy'. The personal, the autobiographical, is nearer yet, although once again the poet herself wrote of the poem in terms which imply a tough detachment, and which force one at least to try to read it so as to distinguish the persona from the personality:

> Here is a poem spoken by a girl with an Electra complex. Her father died while she thought he was God. Her case is complicated by the fact that her father was also a Nazi and her mother very possibly part Jewish. In the daughter the two strains marry and paralyse each other – she has to act out the awful little allegory once over before she is free of it. (Quoted in Rosenthal *The New Poetry*, p 82.)

The poet has also said that, with her own background a mixture of German and Austrian, her 'concern with concentration camps and so on is uniquely intense. And then, again, I'm rather a political person as well, so I suppose that's what part of it comes from.' (Orr *The Poet Speaks*, p 169.)

■   Remembering 'The Colossus', how does 'Daddy' live up to these convictions of both detachment and intense involvement? Do the personal and historical combine to embody some intuition about both?

Daddy

> You do not do, you do not do
> Any more, black shoe
> In which I have lived like a foot
> For thirty years, poor and white,
> Barely daring to breathe or Achoo.
>
> Daddy, I have had to kill you.
> You died before I had time——
> Marble-heavy, a bag full of God,
> Ghastly statue with one grey toe
> Big as a Frisco seal

And a head in the freakish Atlantic
Where it pours bean green over blue
In the waters off beautiful Nauset.
I used to pray to recover you.
Ach, du.

In the German tongue, in the Polish town
Scraped flat by the roller
Of wars, wars, wars.
But the name of the town is common.
My Polack friend

Says there are a dozen or two.
So I never could tell where you
Put your foot, your root,
I never could talk to you.
The tongue stuck in my jaw.

It stuck in a barb wire snare.
Ich, ich, ich, ich,
I could hardly speak.
I thought every German was you.
And the language obscene

An engine, an engine
Chuffing me off like a Jew.
A Jew to Dachau, Auschwitz, Belsen.
I began to talk like a Jew.
I think I may well be a Jew.

The snows of the Tyrol, the clear beer of Vienna
Are not very pure or true.
With my gypsy ancestress and my weird luck
And my Taroc pack and my Taroc pack
I may be a bit of a Jew.

I have always been scared of *you*,
With your Luftwaffe, your gobbledygoo.
And your neat moustache
And your Aryan eye, bright blue.
Panzer-man, panzer-man, O You——

Not God but a swastika
So black no sky could squeak through.
Every woman adores a Fascist,
The boot in the face, the brute
Brute heart of a brute like you.

You stand at the blackboard, daddy,
In the picture I have of you,
A cleft in your chin instead of your foot
But no less a devil for that, no not
Any less the black man who

Bit my pretty red heart in two.
I was ten when they buried you.
At twenty I tried to die
And get back, back, back, to you.
I thought even the bones would do.

But they pulled me out of the sack,
And they stuck me together with glue.
And then I knew what to do.
I made a model of you,
A man in black with a Meinkampf look

And a love of the rack and the screw.
And I said I do, I do.
So daddy, I'm finally through.
The black telephone's off at the root,
The voices just can't worm through.

If I've killed one man, I've killed two——
The vampire who said he was you
And drank my blood for a year,
Seven years, if you want to know.
Daddy, you can lie back now.

There's a stake in your fat black heart
And the villagers never liked you.
They are dancing and stamping on you.
They always *knew* it was you.
Daddy, daddy, you bastard, I'm through.

Discussion

4.4   This is indeed the 'awful little allegory' Sylvia Plath calls it. The basic metaphor this
time is of her father as a Nazi, but also a multitude of evil, folklore figures, the black
man who 'Bit my pretty red heart in two', the vampire with a stake through the
heart; while she, the child-persona, is imagined as a Jew in her relation to him. Her
'Electra complex' lies in the frenzied love-hate elements in the situation (a reminder
of the *Oresteia* referred to in 'The Colossus'). The poem begins with what are now
familiar references to her way of imagining her father, to his massive size, crushing
her in submission, but also to specifically autobiographical detail, such as the 'Polish
town', and her efforts to learn his tongue. From there on, however, the hints of
barbarism and brutality are taken up by means of the Nazi–Jew metaphor, echoing
the repetitious, nursery rhyme effect of 'Lady Lazarus' with an insistent rhyme on
one word all the way through, so as once again to establish a bizarrely appropriate
tone. It is hypnotic, maliciously unpleasant, an attack on the reader. Sylvia Plath
said she could not read aloud her earlier poems, but apparently had no trouble with
this which, with 'Lady Lazarus', she called 'light verse', and then read to Alvarez one
day in a voice 'hot and full of venom'.[4]

The strength of the feeling behind poetry such as this strips it bare of the somewhat
ornate formalities of her earlier verse, reducing it to a long, sinewy, incantatory form,
as if she were a witch casting a spell to bring reality into her fantasy. It is fast, remorse-
less and difficult to resist; it seems to face the worst sadomasochistic impulses which
lie close to every individual, as we know from Freud, and yet to broaden this to
include the revelations of the prison camps. The extremity of suicide, getting back to
her father in the only way she knows, is paralleled by the extremities of Nazi
oppression. Does this work? If it does, it may do so as a reflection adding power to
her image of herself, the personal insight at the centre. George Steiner has said that

[4] Alvarez *The Savage God*, p 32. Listen for yourself on *The Poet Speaks*, No. 5, Argo PLP 1085, recorded
29 August 1962.

'Daddy' achieves 'the classic act of generalisation, translating a private, obviously intolerable hurt into a code of plain statement, of instantaneously public images which concern us all'. But he has also questioned whether someone, herself uninvolved with the horrors thus manipulated long after the event, does not 'commit a subtle larceny' when invoking Auschwitz and appropriating it so readily to a private design. (Steiner 'Dying is an Art' in Newman (ed) *The Art of Sylvia Plath*, p 218.)

Steiner is, in fact, trying to have it both ways, and in the end one must surely decide how one is to respond to such poetry. Does Sylvia Plath bring off the 'classic act of generalisation' or diagnosis making her poem *about* a person, not necessarily herself, although obviously *using* personal experience as a source? And does her daring, control and yet keenness of private feeling then justify such allusions? Or, on the other hand, is the poem really an almost paranoic delusion on her part, a delusion which allows her to identify herself with the suffering of the Jews tortured and massacred in our recent past? I think this is not an easy question to resolve, but it is central to how we finally respond to poems such as 'Daddy' or 'Lady Lazarus'. Naturally, you must make up your own mind after reading the poems.

My own feeling (and I must confess to having felt differently about this at different times) is that, in the end, the poem fails to transcend the terrifyingly personal or 'confessional' element at its centre, and although it remains much more than merely personal in its effect, especially in the way it brings together brutality and love as in some sense connected, deep in our primitive selves, it fails to extend itself through its use of historical allusions. These are, I feel, finally unjustified, not merely a 'subtle larceny', but a blatant fraud. ■

4.5   Sylvia Plath's reputation was largely created by poems such as 'Lady Lazarus' and 'Daddy', published posthumously in *Ariel*, and written in the last few months of her life. While there is an undeniable shift towards a more 'extreme' style – more painfully personal in subject, more shockingly dealt with by means of a radically 'free' and yet disciplined manner – it is possible, I think, to see a continuity with the earlier verse. This continuity is less obvious if one omits the poems written between *The Colossus* and *Ariel* (which can be found in *Crossing the Water*), as I have done, but I hope you will have gathered some sense of its existence in the links between the earlier and the later poems.

4.6   But *Ariel* is not all of a piece with 'Lady Lazarus' or 'Daddy'. Sylvia Plath's abilities are more wide-ranging than the usual concentration on those poems suggests, as I have tried to indicate in my discussion, and this is also evident in such late poems as 'Fever 103°', a Donne-like meditation on the purifying fires of the fevers of sickness and love, playing on the erotic ambiguities of her situation as metaphor with great aplomb. (Discussed by Alvarez in the Course Reader.) There are tender poems, too, such as 'Morning Song' and 'Nick and the Candlestick'. Indeed, 'Nick and the Candlestick', a domestic poem occasioned by her son, shows just how finely her mastery of startling, intricate yet colloquial language can be exploited to a most moving end. And here the personal is finely generalized by means of religious metaphor: love, faith and praise turn this baby into the Christ-child, 'the baby in the barn'.

Nick and the Candlestick

I am a miner. The light burns blue.
Waxy stalactites
Drip and thicken, tears

The earthen womb
Exudes from its dead boredom.
Black bat airs

Wrap me, raggy shawls,
Cold homicides.
They weld to me like plums.

Old cave of calcium
Icicles, old echoer.
Even the newts are white,

Those holy Joes.
And the fish, the fish——
Christ! they are panes of ice,

A vice of knives,
A piranha
Religion, drinking

Its first communion out of my live toes.
The candle
Gulps and recovers its small altitude,

Its yellows hearten.
O love, how did you get here?
O embryo

Remembering, even in sleep,
Your crossed position.
The blood blooms clean

In you, ruby.
The pain
You wake to is not yours.

Love, love,
I have hung our cave with roses,
With soft rugs——

The last of Victoriana.
Let the stars
Plummet to their dark address,

Let the mercuric
Atoms that cripple drip
Into the terrible well,

You are the one
Solid the spaces lean on, envious.
You are the baby in the barn.

5 CONCLUSION

5.1 Again, I do not want to come to any final, definitive judgement here. I hope I have suggested some of the characteristic qualities of Sylvia Plath's work, giving you some idea of its varied but also obsessional qualities, qualities which, for all we know, were only beginning to find their proper form of expression. Ted Hughes has written of his late wife's 'fierce and uncompromising nature', of her 'strange muse, bald, white and wild', but also of her as 'a child desperately infatuated with the world'. (Hughes 'Sylvia Plath' *Poetry Book Society Bulletin*.) Perhaps it is this desperate child which gets through to us in her most famous but angry poems, 'Daddy' and 'Lady Lazarus', yet with the limitations this implies. Her best poems transcend these limitations.

5.2 Thus – and I would like to leave you with this remarkable poem – in 'The Arrival of the Bee Box', for example, her characteristic obsessions are present while at the same time she shows how very aware she could be of the dangers they represented to her – and to others. It is one of several poems she wrote about bee-keeping – 'The Bee-keeper's Daughter' is literally what she was – and while it seems on one level to be about a rather ordinary, everyday event, it is also 'extreme' and 'modern' in tone. The cool, distancing associations of classical allusion which were present in those earlier, more austere poems in *The Colossus* reappear, so that the effect is less of a strident demand for identification and sympathy, but more one of analysis, diagnosis – and humour. As in Hughes's 'Hawk Roosting' perhaps, we are led to identify with the narrator only to realize that the narrator's state of mind is questionable, even evil. For once, Sylvia Plath is not the victim, but the oppressor – and she knows it.

The Arrival of the Bee Box

I ordered this, this clean wood box
Square as a chair and almost too heavy to lift.
I would say it was the coffin of a midget
Or a square baby
Were there not such a din in it.

The box is locked, it is dangerous.
I have to live with it overnight
And I can't keep away from it.
There are no windows, so I can't see what is in there.
There is only a little grid, no exit.

I put my eye to the grid.
It is dark, dark,
With the swarmy feeling of African hands
Minute and shrunk for export,
Black on black, angrily clambering.

How can I let them out?
It is the noise that appals me most of all,
The unintelligible syllables.
It is like a Roman mob,
Small, taken one by one, but my god, together!

I lay my ear to furious Latin.
I am not a Caesar.
I have simply ordered a box of maniacs.
They can be sent back.
They can die, I need feed them nothing, I am the owner.

I wonder how hungry they are.
I wonder if they would forget me
If I just undid the locks and stood back and turned into a tree.
There is the laburnum, its blond colonnades,
And the petticoats of the cherry.

They might ignore me immediately
In my moon suit and funeral veil.
I am no source of honey
So why should they turn on me?
Tomorrow I will be sweet God, I will set them free.

The box is only temporary.

SUGGESTIONS FOR FURTHER WORK ON SYLVIA PLATH

1 Starting with the comparison between Ted Hughes's 'View of a Pig' and Sylvia Plath's 'Sow' you might examine what the two poets have in common, and yet what makes them as 'distinct and different' as their 'fingerprints themselves must be'. ('Blackberrying' and 'Wuthering Heights' in *Crossing the Water* might also be helpful here.)

2 It has been said that most of Sylvia Plath's poems have 'an actable dramatic situation at their root' (Barry Kyle, *Sylvia Plath: A Dramatic Portrait*, Faber, 1976); and the poet herself referred to the characters of the narrators of several of her most well-known poems (most obviously 'Daddy' and 'Lady Lazarus') as if they were distinct from herself. How useful do you find this idea? Look at the well-known poems discussed or referred to in the unit, but also at, say 'Lesbos' (*Winter Trees*) and 'Mirror' (*Crossing the Water*) or other poems which interest you.

3 Robert Lowell wrote of Sylvia Plath: 'In the best poems, one is torn by saying, "This is so true and lived that most other poetry seems like an exercise," and then one can back off and admire the dazzling technique and invention. Perfect control, like the control of a skier who avoids every death-trap until reaching the last drop'. (Rosenthal *The New Poets*, p 68.) Discuss this judgement in the light of what you consider some of Plath's best poems. You might like to start with some reference to Lowell's influence upon her, in particular from the point of view of their shared interest in what Rosenthal labelled 'confessional' verse. In this context, you might look too at the poetry of Anne Sexton and/or John Berryman, especially the latter's *Dream Songs*, 1964, 1968.

4 Sylvia Plath has stated that the issues of our time influence her poetry only 'in a sidelong fashion . . . My poems do not turn out to be about Hiroshima, but about a child forming itself finger by finger in the dark' ('Context', *London Magazine*, new series I, February 1962, p 46). Comment on this in relation to your choice of her poems, starting perhaps with 'Nick and the Candlestick'.

5 Is Sylvia Plath a 'modernist' poet? If so, is this a matter of tone, of technique, or of subject – or of a combination of all of these?

FURTHER READING

Again, as with Ted Hughes, the first and most important thing to do is to read more of her poems. You could look also at her autobiographical novel, *The Bell Jar*. The most useful introductory book that is also easily available is Eileen Aird's *Sylvia Plath*. But the best starting place is the collection of articles, essays, biographical pieces, uncollected poems and bibliographical data edited by Charles Newman, *The Art of Sylvia Plath*.

Sylvia Plath was not a critic in the same sense as Ted Hughes, but she often made revealing comments, on her own background and poetry at least, in interviews such as may be found in 'Context', in *London Magazine*, new series I, February 1962, pp 45–6; 'Ocean 1212-W', *The Listener*, LXX, 29 August 1963, pp 312–13, reprinted in *The Art of Sylvia Plath*; and Peter Orr (ed), *The Poet Speaks* (1966), pp 167–72.

In *The Poet Speaks*, No. 5, Argo PLP 1085, she reads 'Fever 103°', 'Daddy' and 'Lady Lazarus'.

SELECT CRITICISM AND REFERENCES

Aird, Eileen M. (1973) *Sylvia Plath*, Modern Writers Series, Oliver & Boyd.

Alvarez, A. (1968) *Beyond All This Fiddle*, Random House. Contains 'Sylvia Plath', with a postcript from *Tri Quarterly*, 1966, and 'Beyond All This Fiddle'.

Alvarez, A. (1974) *The Savage God*, Penguin.

Cox, C. B. and Jones A. R. 'After the Tranquillized Fifties' *Critical Quarterly* VI (Summer 1964) pp 107–22. Especially good on her relation to Lowell's *Life Studies* and on 'Daddy'.

Hardwick, Elizabeth (1974) *Seduction and Betrayal*, Weidenfeld & Nicholson. Contains 'Sylvia Plath', which examines the self-pitying, even decadent Plath.

Hardy, Barbara 'The Poetry of Sylvia Plath: Enlargement or Derangement?', in Martin Dodsworth (ed) (1970) *The Survival of Poetry*, Faber. Includes a stimulating discussion of 'Nick and the Candlestick'.

Hughes, Ted 'Sylvia Plath' *Poetry Book Society Bulletin*, February 1965.

Jones, A. R. 'Necessity and Freedom: The Poetry of Robert Lowell, Sylvia Plath and Anne Sexton' *Critical Quarterly* VII (January 1965) pp 13–30.

Newman, Charles (ed) (1970) *The Art of Sylvia Plath*, Faber.

Orr, Peter (ed) (1966) *The Poet Speaks*, Barnes & Noble.

Plath, Sylvia (1966) *The Bell Jar*, Faber.

Rosenthal, M. L. (1967) *The New Poets: American and British Poetry Since World War II*, Oxford University Press. Contains a section on Plath as a 'confessional' poet.

Steiner, Nancy Hunter (1974) *A Closer Look at Ariel*, Faber.

ACKNOWLEDGEMENTS

I would like to thank course team colleagues Nick Furbank, Roger Lewis and Graham Martin for helpful and encouraging comments on an earlier draft of this unit; and Mario Relich for time freely given to discuss the poetry of Ted Hughes and Sylvia Plath.

Grateful acknowledgement is also made to Faber and Faber for permission to reprint the following poems by Ted Hughes: 'The Thought-Fox', 'The Jaguar', 'October Dawn' and 'The Hawk in the Rain' from *The Hawk in the Rain*, 1957; 'Hawk Roosting', 'November', 'Thrushes' and 'Pike' from *Lupercal*, 1960; 'Wodwo', 'Theology' and 'Ghost Crabs' from *Wodwo*, 1967; and 'A Childish Prank' from *Crow*, 1970; and to Olwyn Hughes for permission to reprint the following poems by Sylvia Plath: 'Metaphors', 'Two Views of a Cadaver Room', 'The Colossus', 'The Stones' and 'The Disquieting Muses' from *The Colossus* published by Faber and Faber, copyright © 1960 Sylvia Plath, 1967 Ted Hughes; 'Cut', 'You're', 'Lady Lazarus', 'Nick and the Candlestick', 'Daddy' and 'The Arrival of the Bee Box' from *Ariel* published by Faber and Faber, copyright © Ted Hughes, 1965.